Playing for Rang

PLAYING FOR RANGERS NO 18

Edited by Ken Gallacher

Stanley Paul

London Melbourne Auckland Johannesburg

Stanley Paul & Co. Ltd

An imprint of Century Hutchinson Ltd
Brookmount House, 62–65 Chandos Place, Covent Garden,
London WC2N 4NW

Century Hutchinson Australia (Pty) Ltd
PO Box 496, 16–22 Church Street, Hawthorn, Melbourne, Victoria 3122

Century Hutchinson New Zealand Limited
32–34 View Road, PO Box 40–086, Glenfield, Auckland 10

Century Hutchinson South Africa (Pty) Ltd
PO Box 337, Bergvlei 2012, South Africa

First published 1986
© Stanley Paul & Co. Ltd 1986

Set in Baskerville

Phototypeset by Input Typesetting Ltd, London SW19 8DR

Printed in Great Britain by Butler & Tanner Ltd, Frome and London

ISBN 0 09 166171 4

Black and white photographs by Allsport, Colorsport and Sportapics
Colour photographs by Colorsport and Sportapics

Frontispiece: Full back Ally Dawson in action against St Mirren striker
Brian Gallagher

CONTENTS

A BRAVE NEW WORLD AT IBROX!

Early last April Rangers' huge army of fans were preparing themselves for the possibilities . . .

. . . That their heroes would fail to qualify for Europe.

. . . That the Ibrox side would finish their disastrous season with the worst set of League statistics in their history.

. . . And that there seemed little hope of vast improvements being made in time to set the team up for a better season ahead.

Then in stepped the Ibrox chief executive David Holmes and the club chairman John Paton. And the announcement was made which stunned Scottish soccer and sent the name of Rangers echoing around Europe. For Holmes announced to the disbelieving Rangers support that he had signed Scotland World Cup skipper Graeme Souness from the Italian club Sampdoria and had appointed him player-manager.

The one-time Liverpool skipper and midfield general had spent two seasons in Italian football. From there he had returned to play for Scotland, helping guide them to their fourth successive appearance in the finals of the World Cup. It was Souness's inspirational leadership of Scotland which led Holmes to believe that here was the man to rebuild Rangers into a side which would be successful at home in Scotland – and also successful in the wider field of European football.

It was, as former Rangers manager and director Willie Waddell was later to say to me – the most imaginative move in Scottish football for decades.

There had been persistent and powerful rumours that Souness would return to Britain before the end of his three-year contract with the Genoa club. Spurs, the club where he started his career as a youngster, wanted him to go there. Chelsea and West Ham made approaches. Yet all the time that was going on, and the

Soon after the news broke, Graeme Souness sat behind his Ibrox desk for the first time. Beside him are Rangers' Chief Executive David Holmes and Chairman John Paton

A goal in an Old Firm game – and it's for Rangers! A sight the new boss will want to see more of. Ted McMinn scored this one in the 3–0 victory over Celtic in a League game at Ibrox

soccer grapevine was buzzing, Rangers went about their business smoothly and secretly.

They moved in ahead of the English First Division clubs. They set up the deal with Sampdoria which cost them £350,000 to buy Souness. It was only then that the leaks began. In the meantime Jock Wallace, three years in the job, and still with part of his contract to run, had agreed with the board that he

Opposite: Out at Ibrox with one of the impressive new stands behind him, Souness dons a Rangers jersey for the first time. With the new boss is Chairman John Paton
Inset: Portrait of a winner! Souness arrived at Ibrox with medals galore – he wants to add to them

would leave the club. After winning two League Cups, Wallace, the man who had previously won two 'trebles' in his first spell at Ibrox, had found frustrations which had not been there in his earlier reign.

After opening the season well the team had crashed out of the Skol League Cup to Hibs, out of the Scottish Cup to the other Edinburgh team, Hearts, and out of the championship race after topping the table in the first stages of the Premier League battle. It was hard for Wallace to accept – and harder still for the fans who had started the season with hopes high. But the unthinkable had to be faced. Rangers could be out of Europe – and that would mean huge amounts of lost revenue for the club.

Holmes and the board had to act. Yet no-one expected them to act with such boldness. As the big guns in the south talked to Souness about possibilities, Holmes talked to him about the realities of a deal. Counting on the fact that the ex-Anfield captain would be keen to emulate his mate Kenny Dalglish, who was player-manager of Liverpool, Holmes spelled out the chance which waited for him. Souness did not hesitate too long. He discussed the move with his wife and then committed himself to bringing a brave new world to Ibrox.

On the morning that the announcement was made, fans gathered outside the Stadium waiting to catch a glimpse of the new boss. Cars went by honking their horns in salute to the man who had been given the biggest job in Scottish football. Soon afterwards Souness brought in his own number-two, Walter Smith, right-hand man to Dundee United manager Jim McLean and also the assistant to World Cup boss Alex Ferguson. Smith had worked with Souness during the World Cup qualifying games. They had a mutual respect and Smith was able to bring with him a deep knowledge of the game in Scotland which the new man needed to have at his finger tips. It was a partnership which delighted both of the men involved. It also spelled out to the fans that the club were ready to go places.

Money was made available and Souness started laying his plans for the future. He declared that he wanted quality players. He laid down that only top men were required at Ibrox. Winning trophies at home was not to be his only target.

Their ambitions were higher. Souness, one of the soldiers of fortune who had tasted the Italian game, had no wish to stay at home. He wanted Rangers in Europe. It was where they belonged, he maintained. It was there that the fans wanted them to be. With Smith at his side – a man also steeped in European soccer, after years of success at Tannadice – Rangers were

It's Celtic Park this time for an Old Firm clash – something Souness had not savoured until he moved to Rangers. Here Pat Bonner just reaches the ball ahead of Craig Paterson, the Ibrox skipper

clearly in the mood for business.

No rash promises were made. Both men realised that work had to be done, players had to be bought and strategies worked out. But the thinking was BIG. That, most of all, was what pleased the supporters. Within two months of taking up his appointment Souness had paid out almost £800,000 to buy striker Colin West from Watford, and England's number two goalkeeper Chris Woods from Norwich. These were moves which reversed the trend of big money buying in Britain. Rangers were bringing English First Division stars north while always, in the past, the soccer brain drain had been in the opposite direction.

There was a spectacular rush for season tickets put on sale two months earlier than normal. There was a sell-out for a Glasgow Cup Final clash with Celtic which would never normally have attracted over forty thousand fans.

Rangers, the sleeping giants, seemed ready to explode from their slumbers!

MEET THE NEW MANAGER

Thirty-three year old Graeme Souness, recognised as one of the most influential players in Europe, kicked-off a new career when he accepted the job as player-manager of Rangers.

Clearly he was influenced by the impact that his mate Kenny Dalglish made in his first season as boss and player at Anfield. Just as clearly he recognised Rangers as a club which should always be among the most powerful in Europe.

He has always been ambitious. He walked out on Spurs when he was a youngster because he thought he should be in the first team squad. He left Middlesbrough to join Liverpool because he wanted to win honours in the game. And he did so. The only prize he missed in his spell with the Anfield team was an FA Cup medal. Now he wants to keep on winning honours with Rangers.

The sign says it all – Souness is pictured at Ibrox on his first day after being appointed player-boss of Rangers

Kenny Dalglish, Graeme's old Liverpool mate, and the man he turned to for advice when he had the chance of joining Rangers. The success Dalglish had with Liverpool as player-manager helped convince Souness of the importance of that role

Here, talking to editor Ken Gallacher, Souness explains his reasons for taking the job. And outlines what he hopes to achieve. . . .

GALLACHER: Did you always have ambitions to go into management when your playing career was going to end?
SOUNESS: Funnily enough, I didn't always have thoughts about the coaching side of the game. It was only in the past year or two that I realised that I wanted to stay in football. I suppose that when you are coming into your thirties and you know that you don't have too many years left as a player, that's when it hits you. That's when you start to wonder about what you will do without football in your life. Remember I haven't

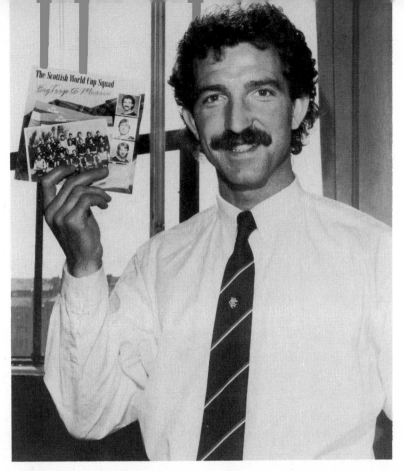

The Scotland skipper too! That's the triple role from Souness – player and manager with Rangers, captain of Scotland. Here he is with the Scots' Mexico squad record

really known anything else since I was a youngster. It would be a difficult job trying to fill that kind of gap in your life.

GALLACHER: What did you feel when you first learned about the Rangers offer?

SOUNESS: I didn't believe it was possible at first. I mean, there had been all the speculation in the Italian press – and here at home too – about Spurs and Chelsea and Arsenal and all the rest. Then out of the blue, in came Rangers. When the Sampdoria President let me know that Rangers wanted me then really, no one else had any chance.

GALLACHER: Why was that? After all, the other clubs are big, glamorous clubs and normally players who have spent their careers in England don't rate the game in Scotland too much.

SOUNESS: That's as maybe. If you're right then I am an obvious exception to that rule. Maybe it's because I used to watch Rangers when I was still at school in Edinburgh. Or maybe it's just because I know the potential of the club.

Remember when I was with Liverpool I played at Ibrox when one of the new stands was opened, so I knew what the set up was like. It's one of the best stadiums in Europe. It has to be. I know the support is there just waiting for success to come along – and it has surprised me that over the past few years Rangers haven't done better in Europe. OK, I realise that sometimes you can draw a tough club in the opening rounds and out you go. That can happen to any team – but it can't happen season after season.

It didn't seem right to me that Aberdeen and Dundee United, with fewer resources than Rangers and Celtic, should be doing better than them in the European competitions. It can be hard in Europe, very hard. But that is where teams make big, big reputations. And big, big money. It is the arena where Rangers should always be competing.

GALLACHER: You must have been very relieved, then, when the team managed to qualify on that last League day.

The vast Rangers support who will see Souness as their Messiah. Here they celebrate a 3–0 win over Old Firm rivals Celtic – they want to celebrate even more with the new men in charge

SOUNESS: You're right. It was essential for us to get into Europe. Unthinkable that we should miss out. If you look back at that day incidentally, it proved to me the kind of support which is available for the team. Celtic won the title at Paisley while Hearts lost it at Dundee. These were two critical games being played on the very last day of the Premier League season. And yet we had a bigger crowd at Ibrox that afternoon than either of the other two matches. If I had had any doubts, the fans that day removed them. But I didn't have any. This is a really big club.

GALLACHER: How big do you think the club is, then? You have been around a bit. You've been with Spurs and Liverpool and had two years in Italy with Sampdoria. Where do you place Rangers alongside them – or alongside any of the other major British and Continental sides?

SOUNESS: They are a bigger outfit than any of the teams you have mentioned. I think they are bigger than Liverpool. Bigger than Spurs or even Arsenal and way ahead of Sampdoria. In Britain the one club who are possibly bigger are Manchester United. I've always felt that Rangers should be up there along-side United and Barcelona and Real Madrid and Roma and Juventus. Whenever anyone talks of top teams in Europe then Rangers should be mentioned. I have always thought that – now I would like to help make that happen. It is not an easy job. I would be telling lies if I didn't admit to being nervous about things when I first accepted the offer. But I knew that this was an opportunity which was too good to turn down and one which might never be repeated.

GALLACHER: You did have other offers from clubs in England – were they tempting?

SOUNESS: As I said earlier, when Rangers came in then the other clubs were wasting their time. But before that the offers from Spurs and Chelsea and West Ham – as well as one or two other teams were tempting. The life was good in Italy but you get a hankering to get home again after two years away.

I suppose it would have been good to go back to Spurs where I blotted my copybook a little when I was a youngster, and do something for them. But this is the job I would have chosen above any other. I still feel very lucky that I was given the chance.

GALLACHER: How do you mean you 'blotted your copybook' at Spurs?

SOUNESS: That's an old, old story now. But all that happened was that as a teenager I thought I should have been in the Spurs first team along with the big names like Dave Mackay.

Graeme's World Cup colleague Davie Cooper

The manager, Bill Nicholson, thought differently. He knew that I had a lot of hard work to do before I could reach first-team standard. I couldn't accept that so I walked out on the club and went back to Edinburgh.

Then, after going back to London, I was sold to Middlesbrough. It was there that Jack Charlton helped save my career. He gave me a hard time. He spelled out to me how hard I had to work at the game and how essential it was to concentrate on football during your career because the playing career is a short one. Big Jack hammered me – and he was right to do it. I became a better player. And that's why Liverpool eventually came in to buy me and give me the best playing years of my life.

GALLACHER: Those were tremendous days for you at Anfield . . . winning all those titles and European Cups. Can that be repeated with Rangers?

SOUNESS: That has to be our aim. It's not going to happen overnight because it didn't happen that way with Liverpool. There are years and years of hard work and experience at Anfield. That is what has made the club so strong. The set up there is thoroughly professional. Just ask anyone in football about Anfield and you will get the same answer. There's nothing too fancy, nothing secret, it's just good solid football common sense. They are very down-to-earth on the backroom staff. You don't hear too much of the coaching jargon around the place. They talk language that players understand and appreciate. Coaches come from all over Europe to see them training, hoping to pick up some fabulous secret. There really isn't one. It's all built on the right basics and on the right people. I'd like to do the same at Ibrox.

But I'm not in the business of making promises too soon. There is a job to do here and we have been told – Walter Smith and myself – that we will be given time to do the job. I have been very impressed by the men in charge at Ibrox. They are as ambitious as I am. They want the club to live up to the reputation it has built through all the previous years of success. But all of us are aware that you cannot rely on tradition all the time. We will have to forge our own tradition.

The earlier we can start to do that the better for everyone connected with the club. However, basic guidelines have to be laid down. The foundations must be put down properly just the way they were at Liverpool years ago.

GALLACHER: Will you try to build the new Rangers in Liverpool's image, so to speak?

SOUNESS: Not exactly. But when you see a successful pattern of training, playing and administration you cannot ignore it. If you do then you are making a mistake. There are things from Liverpool that we can adopt and there are things that Walter and myself will have of our own. Then there are things about the club, and about playing in the Premier League, which have to be taken into account.

So it won't necessarily be a carbon copy of Liverpool – but we will try to use some of their basic ideas and build from there. It would be nice if we could copy their success, mind you!

GALLACHER: Going back to the days when you were a schoolboy in Edinburgh, did you come to see Rangers very often?

SOUNESS: My brother used to bring me along. It's funny that

The man who took Souness to Ibrox – Chief Executive David Holmes wearing his Rangers blazer

down through the years people in Scotland seem to have looked upon me as a Hearts supporter. Probably that's because I come from Edinburgh. But I used to be brought through for some of the big European games. They were marvellous occasions and I remember coming to watch players like Dave Smith, John Greig and Willie Henderson. Those nights have always stayed in my memory.

The stadium was bigger then and the crowds were always huge for the top European attractions. It was very exciting to come along as a kid and see all these great players and be a part of that kind of atmosphere. I think that Dave Smith always impressed me because of the way he tried to play football. He tried to build things from the back at a time when most Scottish teams simply tried to get the ball up the park as quickly as possible. Back then I dreamed about maybe playing for Rangers but they didn't come in for me. Spurs did and that was it. I didn't think, until the offer came last season, that I'd ever get the chance of playing at Ibrox – far less managing the club! It's a dream that I never, ever, thought would become reality.

GALLACHER: Now that it is a reality how do you see yourself settling into a player-manager's role? People have suggested that it's too much for a player at top level to do, though someone proved them all wrong last season!

SOUNESS: You mean Kenny, of course. If I can do half as well as Kenny did in his first season as player-boss then I'll be happy! Dalglish is extraordinary. I cannot say too much about him. The only way he has upset me is by getting to that FA Cup Final last season and winning a medal. After all the years we were there together we never did get beyond a semi-final place and I don't have an English Cup medal.

You're right, there were a few people who thought the job would be too big. There will be people who will say the same about me. I'm quite sure of that. But I talked to Kenny about the Rangers offer before I accepted it. He didn't have to persuade me to take it or anything like that. I knew that I wanted the job. I knew what I wanted to do but it's always nice when you are making a major career decision to have someone to talk it over with. I think we are all the same. You need someone who has been over the course before to talk to. That's what I did with Kenny and very soon he gave me the kind of answers that I had been hoping to get all along. Quite apart from the fact that he had been operating as a player-manager at Liverpool, he is a Glaswegian, and he never lets anyone forget that. And he was once a Rangers supporter which helped him to know what he was talking about when I started to quiz him. He underlined all the things I knew already – that the club was one of the biggest in the game. That they have a fantastic support. And that anyone who can make them great again will be able to fill that marvellous stadium week after week. That has to be the kind of situation that we are aiming for!

GALLACHER: To do that I suppose you have to give the fans the kind of personality players that they want – and that means spending money at times. I know that you have shown your willingness to do that already but have there been any barriers imposed by the directors?

SOUNESS: No, none at all. When I took over, the assurances were given to me about money being made available to streng-

Graeme Souness in action for Sampdoria. The Ibrox boss shows his determination to ward off the challenge from an Italian rival

then the team. It was also spelled out that I could compete with any club in Britain as far as fees and as far as personal terms for players were concerned. I couldn't ask for any more than that.

I went ahead on that assumption and I'll continue that way. We are not limited to players in Scotland. Or Ireland, or England. We have the chance to go anywhere in Europe for the men we might want. This club thinks big. They don't want to be rich and powerful only here at home. They want what I want – to be among Europe's élite. But we're also aware that getting the right team together isn't just about buying players.

I know it goes back to what you said about 'personality players' for the fans. But you must get the blend right. Buying players sensibly is a really important part of things. Plus, being able to get the best young players here at home and bringing them up inside the club learning good habits all the way through from the youth team to the first team. It's all got to come together for us to get the success we want.

GALLACHER: I understand that – but Liverpool have always been a club who are ready to buy players to stay at the top. Would that influence you?

SOUNESS: Perhaps a little bit. It's true that when you get to the top you want to stay there and sometimes that doesn't give you time to bring through as many home grown youngsters as you would like. The thing is that, at Liverpool, the European Cup wins and the title wins put the club on a very strong financial footing. Rangers made money available to me when I took the job as team boss. However, I know that I simply cannot keep on going to the club looking for more and more money to spend on players without being able to generate that cash through the turnstiles. To get that means getting success on the field – or at least proving to the support that we are heading in the right direction. It has to be a two-way thing and I'm very aware of that.

GALLACHER: Who have you turned to for advice on being a manager?

SOUNESS: I spoke to Bill Nicholson who was my first manager when I was down at Spurs because I knew that I would get good, sound advice from him. Similarly I talked to Joe Fagan and Bob Paisley who had been the two bosses I played under during my years at Liverpool. Look, eventually I have to do things my own way. That is essential. You can't do the job the way other people would do it. But it is important to learn a little about the problems and the pitfalls, and to pick up hints from three men who were among the best in the business seemed right for me.

Also, naturally, I have had invaluable advice from Walter Smith on the other teams and players in the Premier League. It would have been almost impossible to come up to the job without a right-hand man who knew the Scottish scene inside out. Walter knows everything there is to know because of the years he spent at Tannadice. Also he had long spells with the Scotland youth team, with the Under-21 team and as coach to the full international side. It's marvellous for me that I have someone like him to fill me in on essential details. After all, while I looked for the Scottish results and met the players from the Premier League who were in the national team, I didn't see Scottish soccer on a regular basis at all. Picking up on the teams and players has been a part of the learning process for me.

Cool it, guys. The Rangers manager leaves no-one in any doubt in his role as Scotland captain

GALLACHER: I suppose that it's important too, to have someone you trust and respect off the field when you are to be so heavily involved on the playing side still.

SOUNESS: Oh, yes, that has to be important. Down at Liverpool Kenny still has Bob there for some of the time at least and the backroom staff hasn't changed very much over the years. Kenny has gone out of his way to say how much he owes to them for helping him settle in during his first season. Again, this is a situation similar to mine where I am playing as well. People off the field can so often see things better than the players. As a player-manager you have to be prepared for that.

GALLACHER: Regarding your playing career and how long it might continue. Have you given much thought to that?

SOUNESS: Everyone I have spoken to says that you always know when it is time to pack in. Equally a whole lot of ex-players have told me that they chucked it too soon. I think in Britain there has always been a thing about players going down-hill immediately they hit thirty or thirty-one. That's not true and it's never been a theory which has gained much acceptance in Europe. I feel good and I feel fit and if that continues then I'd see myself playing for two, maybe three, years. It could be that I'd move back a step.

Instead of staying in the midfield role that I've always played in I could drop back into the back four. Older players have often done that. Just drop back a little when you begin to feel that you might need a little more time to do things. That's what's in my mind at the moment. But you never know exactly how things will work out. I do know that before going to Mexico we had very rigorous fitness tests from the SFA doctor because of the problems that altitude would give us in the World Cup Finals. We all got the reports sent to us and I was as fit as anyone in the party of twenty-two who went there last summer. So even though I'm maybe getting on a bit it doesn't mean that I have to hang up my boots when I reach a certain age. I do believe that I'll know when the time comes. I'll know within myself when training becomes a chore or playing becomes too much. When that happens then I'll step out of the side and concentrate on management. But that's very much in the future the way I feel at the present. When I took the job I told Rangers that I wanted to do a job for them on the field as well as off the field. That was my intention then. It's my intention now. And it will remain my intention until I find myself in the situation where I am forced to stop playing. I'll know when that is. No one will have to tell me!

GALLACHER: If you had your time over would you have

preferred to join Rangers as a schoolboy, play for them and then take over? Or do you think this is the best way for you and for the club?

SOUNESS: I think it's probably better this way. If you are at one club and one club only then you could possibly have a blinkered view of the game. That's my opinion, anyhow. For some people that could be OK – but not for me. I have been around a little bit. I've played at the top level in England and in Italy and now in Scotland. I have played in the European Cup and won that trophy with Liverpool. I've played in three World Cups with Scotland. Now some of that experience would still have been with me if I'd been at Ibrox and nowhere else – but not all of it.

What I have learned from my career can be used to help the players with Rangers (hopefully) become better players. Similarly, Walter Smith has a tremendous pedigree as assistant manager to Jim McLean at Dundee United. What he has learned there and in Europe will be used to help this club. If both of us had grown up inside the club and never been away then I doubt if the kind of experience we have would have been there. I believe very strongly in the European experience and both of us have that.

GALLACHER: It comes through very strongly that Europe is where it is all happening for you – is that a fair assessment of your views?

SOUNESS: Very much so. To get into Europe you must be successful at home in the domestic competitions. To get into the European Cup – which has to be our eventual aim – you must win the title. So if it looks a priority it is because you get success at home first and then go into Europe looking for more.

Europe is the stage, make no mistake about that. That is the stage where I enjoy performing and where Rangers should always be on show. They need the kind of platform that Europe offers the really big clubs. They have to be there alongside all the other glittering names from the Continent. I want to get back to the days when Rangers were mentioned in the same breath as Real Madrid and Barcelona. As Juventus and Inter Milan. As Bayern Munich and Hamburg. As Anderlecht and Standard Liège.

That is where they belong. It's my job to put them back there. And then to keep them there. It won't be achieved inside a few months but I hope it will be achieved, and if it's down to hard work and ambition on my part then we'll get there. It's where Rangers want to be. And it's where I want to be as well. . . .

THE NIGHT THAT THE RAINS CAME DOWN

That European jinx which has persisted so cruelly over the past seven years struck Rangers yet again last season. Again the Ibrox side crashed out of a European tournament in the first round and the supporters who 'follow, follow' so passionately were left casting their minds back to the last time their team had gone as far as the quarter-finals. That was back in the 1978–79 season when in John Greig's first year as manager they made an epic challenge for the European Cup – the trophy they have wanted so desperately to win for so many seasons.

In the first round that year the mighty Juventus, champions of Italy, and the side which provided the bulk of Italy's World Cup squad in Argentina a few months earlier, were defeated. Their stars were unable to cope with the aggression of Rangers over the two legs. And in the second round the talented Dutchmen of PSV Eindhoven suffered the same fate. They, too, had a clutch of World Cup aces. The van der Kerkof twins were there, the men who did so much to take Holland to the Finals in Buenos Aires a few months earlier. Once more, though, Rangers matched them, outplayed them and then went into the quarter-finals.

But from that time until now there have been few famous victories. No long runs through to the later stages of whatever tournaments the club has qualified for – and little for the fans to celebrate. Last season, when the men from Ibrox were drawn against the little known Spanish team Real Osasuna, hopes rose. It was the kind of draw the fans liked. Enough of a challenge because the team did play in the Spanish First Division – but hopefully, not too much of a challenge in only the first round of the UEFA Cup!

The fans like a team tinged with glamour instead of someone who may prove a walkover but not provide them with anything like the atmosphere of a big European occasion at Ibrox. The Spaniards seemed to fit the bill perfectly. They came from a strong footballing nation. Rangers had had glamour packed clashes with other Spanish teams down through their European

Cammy Fraser tries to beat the Spanish goalkeeper to the ball in the mudbath of Ibrox when Real Osasuna provided the opposition in their European tie

history. And the fact that few people knew anything about Osasuna suggested that the second round could be a reality for the Scots.

Nostalgia, always such an important ingredient when it comes to talking about European games, played an important part in getting the atmosphere right for the first-leg game at Ibrox. Supporters could go back to games against Real Madrid and Real Zaragoza. Games against Atletico Bilbao, Valencia and Seville. They could think back to the great players who had played in these matches. To Puskas and Canario and Iribar and Kempes.

Real Osasuna didn't have any big names but they did come from Spain and they did become identified in the minds of the supporters with all these great names and great games of the past. Enough to bring a crowd of thirty thousand into Ibrox on the night that the rains came down and almost caused the game to be postponed. . . .

Before that however, before the shock weather which hit the match, there had been other shocks for the huge Ibrox support. Twenty-four hours before the game Manager Jock Wallace named his team and incredibly, in such a short time, there were only three survivors of the last team to play in Europe for Rangers. That was only ten months earlier when a determined barrage at Ibrox was almost enough to carry Rangers through against the powerful men from Inter Milan. A crushing first-leg defeat seemed to have ended the side's hopes then – but the magnificent comeback at Ibrox brought them within a goal of qualifying for the next round of the tourney.

It remained a heart-warming memory – but only three players were around to share thoughts of that night. The survivors, when Manager Jock Wallace announced his team from their training HQ at Dunblane, were Craig Paterson, Dave McPherson and Cammy Fraser. At that time Rangers were going strongly in the League and Wallace issued a battle cry to the fans.

Bad luck as well as bad weather struck Rangers in the tie. Here, with the Spaniards under siege, Derek Johnstone's header strikes the post and rebounds clear. That effort could have taken Rangers into the second round . . .

Centre half Craig Paterson rises from the mud to be congratulated by Ally McCoist and Davie Cooper after scoring the one goal of the game with a diving header in the teeming rain of Ibrox

'The supporters have been fantastic this season. They have been right behind the team. All season they have given us the kind of backing that players respond to. The kind of backing which makes opposition teams nervous. That is important at any time. It will be even more important for this game because Osasuna are playing in European football for the first time. They must be nervous enough in any case – let's make them more nervous with an old style Ibrox welcome!'

The Wallace strategy was to look for goals coming from the midfield with comeback man Cammy Fraser earmarked as a possible scorer. It was from that area the Rangers manager

Right back Hugh Burns – one of the stars of the storm. Here he crosses the ball as a Spanish defender slides in too late to stop him

wanted to win the tie, and to win it by enough goals to make the second leg a formality.

The Spaniards, meanwhile, were edgy and more than a little apprehensive as they prepared for their début in a Continental competition. Their Yugoslav coach Ivan Brzic had decided that the man he must fear most of all in the Rangers line-up was winger Davie Cooper, the sole Scotland World Cup man in the side. He admitted beforehand: 'Our aim has to be to keep the score down. To do that we must try to shackle Cooper, to stop him before he can make the ammunition for the Rangers front men. If we can do that with any kind of success then we will have a chance when we get Rangers back to our own ground. It is smaller than Ibrox. Our players like it there. They are used to it and maybe Rangers won't enjoy it as much as they do their own huge stadium. That is what we hope at any rate. . . .'

At the end of the ninety minutes the Spanish unknowns from Pamplona, a town more famous for the running of bulls than for soccer, achieved the result they wanted. But they did not do so entirely by their own efforts. Instead they were helped by a deluge which turned Ibrox into a quagmire. Pools of water lay everywhere as the new drainage system attempted to cope with extraordinary rain. In normal circumstances the game would have been postponed and been played the following night. But somehow the referee made the decision to go ahead – and even as conditions worsened as the night wore on he stuck to that decision.

Postponements have happened before in Europe and there was the time at Ibrox when heavy snow caused the European Cup quarter-final tie with Cologne to be put off for twenty-four hours. It was then played on the Thursday night – this time that option wasn't on offer!

And so Rangers were forced to try for their commanding lead in farcical conditions. The Spaniards laid out their stall to defend and, with the help of the conditions, they were able to do that. It was not the kind of night which lent itself to quick attacking play. Passes were held up in the giant puddles which formed on the playing surface. It was impossible for players to judge how the ball would react when it struck the watery pitch. And impossible for anyone to know where it might end up as it skidded from boots or heads – it was a nightmare for everyone. Yet, even in these conditions, almost thirty thousand people were at the match willing Rangers to victory.

A victory did arrive, but not by the convincing margin that Jock Wallace had wanted. Nor by a margin that Rangers would need in the return leg in Spain.

At the end of ninety sodden, dripping, dreadful minutes Rangers had won by just one solitary goal. That had come in the ninth minute of the second-half and, while it did not come from the midfield as Wallace had hoped, it did come from the back of the team. From skipper Craig Paterson whose gallant diving header inside the penalty area left the Spanish defenders stranded. The central defender was up joining the attack when Hugh Burns swung a free-kick into the goalmouth. Not one of the Spanish players could compete with Paterson's courage as he hurled himself forward to reach the ball and guide it into the net.

It was an important goal on a night when little went right for Rangers' attacking plans. The so talented midfield of Dougie Bell, Robert Russell and Cammy Fraser became bogged down in the mud. And after the goal arrived to break the seeming deadlock, Wallace took off two of his attackers, Bobby Williamson and Davie Cooper. Just a week earlier Cooper's penalty kick goal in Cardiff had helped Scotland towards Mexico. Now he was taken off to jeers from the fans.

Yet the double substitution almost paid off as the Scots battled for more goals. Ted McMinn replaced Cooper and Derek Johnstone came on for Williamson to add his aerial strength to the attacks. Paterson's goal had suggested that Osasuna might be vulnerable to that kind of scoring effort – and it proved that way. Johnstone wreaked havoc as Rangers piled on pressure towards the end of the game. He saw one header strike a post and another, delicately placed in the path of fellow sub McMinn, almost brought that elusive second.

Afterwards Wallace explained his changes. He pointed out: 'We found it hard to get the ball out to Davie Cooper because of the conditions. They were among the worst I've ever known in any game. When we did manage to get the ball out wide to him he had problems running with it. I had to make changes and when Johnstone came on he had four magnificent headers. He was terribly unlucky not to score at least one goal. He deserved that for the work he put in and the trouble he caused their defence. The real problem for us was not their defence – but the weather. That made it hard to attack and it suited them. They were happy to sit back and they didn't have to make too many passing moves in conditions which held up the ball all the time.

'We can still win in Spain because we saw where we could cause them problems. They didn't like it when the crosses flew into their penalty box. It's up to us to exploit that weakness once more.'

Striker Bobby Williamson was brought on in the second leg as
Rangers tried for the one goal they needed to take them into the
next round. Here he jousts with ex-Ibrox player Kenny Black of Hearts

Wallace's optimism, though, was matched by that of Brzic who had come expecting the worst – and then found himself in a commanding position in a tie which had been so nearly washed out. Smiling afterwards he summed up the game by saying: 'The match was more physical than I thought it would be. Maybe the conditions helped to cause that. Really the rain has left me bewildered. I know no more about Rangers now than I did before the kick-off. It was impossible to judge any team or any players.

'But I do know one thing – Cooper is still the man we fear most of all. It is up to Rangers that they took him off and not for me to say anything about it. But in Spain we must be careful about Cooper. Still, now we believe we can win the tie – and that will be a big boost to football in our town. Never before

A powerful header from Craig Paterson clears this ball – but he was less fortunate in Spain where defensive errors gave Osasuna both their goals

Another of the men who were blamed in Spain – Dave McPherson. Here he jumps along with Celtic striker Mark McGhee

have we been in Europe and, drawn against a team with a big reputation in our country, we thought that we would go out immediately. Now we can march on!'

The problems for Rangers continued after that match. It kicked off their worst spell of the season till then – with four successive defeats looming. Immediately following that first leg they lost to Dundee at Ibrox; then in the League Cup they went down 2–0 in the first leg of the semi-final againt Hibs. And as a prelude to their trip to Spain they lost another home Premier League game to Aberdeen by a score of 3–0. Not only that but Hugh Burns and Craig Paterson were both ordered off and a furious row broke out as Wallace lashed Aberdeen players for 'feigning injury'.

It was scarcely the build up required for a hazardous trip to the bull-fight centre of Pamplona. Once there, though, Wallace began his bid to raise the team's battered morale. He announced the team twenty-four hours in advance with a flourish of confidence as he tried to undermine the confidence of Osasuna. Derek Johnstone was recalled to lead the attack with a boost from Wallace. Said the Ibrox manager: 'Derek has unmatched experience of these European occasions plus he worried the Spanish defence when he came on in the first leg. As well as that he is in line for a run in the first team. He was outstanding in the reserves at Pittodrie in midfield. He'll play here as a striker and he will come into the first team at centre-half back home because Craig Paterson is suspended. He has the chance to establish himself in the first team again. It's up to him.'

Wallace retained Davie Cooper – knowing that he, too, worried the Spaniards. And he gave Iain Durrant his European début in midfield. Originally the youngster was to play in the first leg but the cruelly demanding conditions had meant he was left out. Now came his chance!

There was a sell-out crowd in the twenty-six thousand capacity El Sadar Stadium on a warm Spanish night; the temperature at kick-off time was nudging its way into the seventies. It was a perfect night for football – but it stayed that way as far as Rangers were concerned for just twelve short minutes. That's how long it took for their so fragile lead to disappear. A cross into goal found Paterson and his partner Dave McPherson lost and, as the two six-footers failed to clear, the little Spanish skipper Ripodas sneaked into the space left for him, took his time and headed the ball into the net. It was a body blow for the Scots who had hoped to frustrate their opponents for the opening twenty minutes and then gradually begin to stretch out and look for a vital away goal themselves. Those kind of tactics had been employed successfully before and Rangers wanted to repeat them. Osasuna had other ideas as the Ripodas header proved . . . and as their attacking flurries continued to prove.

As Davie Cooper, the hoped-for ace card for the Ibrox team stuttered and stammered his way through the match against the close-marking defence, Osasuna had their own wing wizard. Their one international, Martin, who had missed the first leg of the tie at Ibrox, returned and proceeded to torture the Ibrox defence. His crosses caused constant danger. His runs were a continual threat. And in the fortieth minute he became the scorer of the second goal for the Basque side. Again it was a cross which created the danger with Martin's wing partner

The unorthodox Ted McMinn, another sub in Spain when Rangers
were down by two goals in the second leg of their UEFA Cup game

Benito sending the ball over.

Again the defence failed to react to the menace which was all too obvious to the few hundred Scots fans who had travelled to see Rangers in action.

Iain Durrant who made his European début in Pamplona

And again the ball ended in the net and now the Spaniards were winning the tie and Rangers were on the rack. Yet, strangely enough, it was then when they were in trouble that the Scots began to reach a performance peak. With half an hour remaining they took control of the game. The nerve of the Spanish players began to go. They knew that they were living on a knife edge. Winning the tie by 2–1 but with the knowledge that one goal from Rangers – with the away goals counting double in European competitions – would put them out of the tournament!

It was a dramatic closing thirty minutes as Rangers made substitutions in an attempt to get that single goal which would change the whole result of the tie and carry them forward into the second round of the UEFA Cup.

Off again went World Cup star Davie Cooper with Bobby Williamson replacing him in an effort to add to the firepower going through the hearts of the Osasuna defence . . . off went Robert Russell with the unpredictable Ted McMinn coming on to take his place, running at the Spanish defenders, hoping to find a way through for the single goal which was needed.

But it didn't come, and Rangers were left contemplating what might have been. It was the same sad, sorry story of their recent adventures into Europe. An early KO and recriminations to follow. The cruellest statistic of all for the team to face was that they had gone four games now without scoring. The last goal they had managed had come in the first leg of the UEFA Cup tie at Ibrox!

Afterwards Jock Wallace ruefully commented: 'The game kicked off at eight-thirty p.m. but we didn't start playing until half past nine! It was a bad start by us. Let's be honest, we should be a better team than Osasuna over two games but here, on the night, we were not.

'Instead we were left with an uphill battle in that second half. Losing two goals the way we did was criminal. We had wanted to cool things down, take our time and defend sensibly for the first half hour or so. It didn't happen that way and we were punished for mistakes. After half-time we might have scored given a bit of luck. But right now luck is not with us.'

So Rangers were left counting the cost of an early exit from Europe again. This time at the hands of a team who, later in the season, escaped relegation from the Spanish First Division by the narrowest of margins. The defeat was a disaster financially. And an even bigger disaster in terms of European prestige, already fast fading away!

'I'VE ALWAYS BEEN A RANGER,' says Walter Smith

The appointment of thirty-eight year old Walter Smith as assistant manager to player-boss Graeme Souness may not have grabbed the headlines in the same devastating way as the manager's return from Italy. But in the game itself it was hailed as another coup by the ambitious Ibrox board. The man who had been at Jim McLean's right hand with Dundee United during their best years was widely recognised as one of the best coaches in the country.

On other occasions, when clubs had tried to woo him away from Tannadice, his mentor, McLean, had persuaded him to stay. It seemed certain that when the Tannadice boss decided to give up active management then Smith would step in to maintain the continuity at one of the most progressive provincial clubs in the country.

Among others, Motherwell had wanted him as manager. Smith, though, remained with United where he was the highest paid number-two in Scotland. And last season United made it clear how highly they regarded him by appointing him a director of the club. That meant he joined Jim McLean on the board and United became the only team in the country with their manager and assistant manager also directors of the club.

None of that, though, was enough to keep Smith at Tannadice when the approach from Rangers came. The Ibrox club, scrupulous to the last in their dealings with United, made the approach to Tannadice chairman George Fox. Then, once permission was given to speak to Smith, they went ahead and soon, the coach who had supported Rangers as a boy, had joined the new Ibrox set-up.

It was a chance he thought had been lost two and a half years earlier when Jim McLean was asked to be Rangers' manager before any offer was made to Jock Wallace to return.

Towards the end of last season he revealed to me: 'When Rangers made their offer to Jim he was set to take the job – and he told me that he wanted me to go to Ibrox with him. It was strange that day. It was a Monday morning, I'll never forget it. Jim had gone to Ibrox to speak to the directors there and take a look at the set-up.

When he arrived at the ground for training the next morning he took me aside and told me: "I'm going to take the job and I want you to come with me as assistant manager."

'I couldn't believe it. It was something I'd always dreamed about, going to Rangers, I mean.

'Jim then went up to see the chairman to discuss the details of moving to Ibrox and into the new job. I went into the dressing

One-time Dundee United coach Walter Smith, and now Rangers and Scotland number two, makes a point in a training session on the beach

room, sat down to read the newspapers and try to gather my thoughts. Not too long afterwards one of the other directors came downstairs from the boardroom into the dressing room and announced that Jim had decided to stay with United. He was going on about how it was great news for the club, and I was sitting there wondering what had happened to keep me away from the job I wanted above all others!

'But Jim, you see, had had a very good relationship with the chairman, the late Johnstone Grant. It was Mr Grant who talked him into staying and when Jim stayed I stayed too. It was a real disappointment because, quite honestly, I thought that would be the one and only chance which would come my way. It isn't very often in life that you get another opportunity to fulfil an ambition when one has come up and been lost.'

Smith's love affair with Rangers began when he was just five years old and his grandfather took him to Ibrox to see them play Queens Park in a First Division match. That was back in 1953 and from that time on Smith was a fan.

He recalls: 'I can remember that first game because it was Queens Park and they were in the old First Division then. But I cannot remember too much about it otherwise or about the players who took part in the match. I was only about five years old, maybe I was still only four!

'But my grandfather believed in starting me off young and he used to take me to all the games. He helped run the Rangers Supporters' Club at Carmyle where we lived and so every week I went off with him in the supporters' bus to see the team play.

'I kept that up, scarcely missing a match until I started to play football myself. But, then, I still picked up on all the big European games. These were great nights at Ibrox, huge crowds, star players – and always the hope that Rangers would be able to lift one of the major European prizes. I can remember going to see Eintracht Frankfurt, Fiorentina, Red Star Belgrade, Inter Milan and all the rest. Honestly, they were marvellous nights. You would get something like eighty thousand fans into Ibrox for these games back then. I loved them. They were good Rangers teams, too. You had that forward line of Scott, McMillan, Millar, Brand and Wilson. Then Willie Henderson came in and behind them there was Jim Baxter.

'These were class players. Any one of them would have been able to command a place in any of the big name teams they were playing against at the time. Baxter was the biggest name, the star of the team if you like and everyone loved him.

'We all used to stand on the terracings and admire everything he did. What a great player he was. But, it's funny, it's not

One of the men Smith knows from his Scotland role, winger Davie
Cooper, seen here moving away from Welsh defender Robbie
James in the World Cup clash in Cardiff

Top level conference at a Scotland training session. World Cup boss
Alex Ferguson talks things over with Rangers' new number two,
and his own World Cup right-hand man, Walter Smith

always the best player who becomes your favourite. So the
player I had up there on a pedestal was Jimmy Millar. He
typified Rangers for me and for so many of the other fans.
Someone once called him the Lion of Ibrox and that was about
right. That summed him up.

'Jimmy Millar was an old fashioned centre-forward. He led
the line well, he scored goals regularly and he never, ever gave
up. What a battler he was and what a good, good player. He
used to frighten some of these Continental defences. They would
do anything to stop him. They'd kick him, and punch him and
spit at him and Jimmy would just get on with the game. It took
a lot to stop him when he was in full cry. And later when he
dropped back again to what had been his original wing-half
position he was still able to do a job for the team. I used to
think he was one of the all-time great Rangers players – and
still do today. These memories can never be taken away. . . .'

That was Walter's grounding at Ibrox. His education as a
Rangers supporter. These were the glory days at Ibrox; when
Rangers were winning trophies regularly, their players formed
the backbone of the Scotland international squads, and they
were regularly into the quarter-finals or semi-finals or even,
once, the Final of one of the major European tournaments.

Smith's own playing career started to pick up. He joined the crack Glasgow junior side, Ashfield, and soon the powerfully built wing-half was attracting attention from senior scouts. He was invited down south for training by Leicester City and Aston Villa. Then Dundee United asked him to go to Tannadice. Smith waited and waited and wondered if Rangers would come in. But they didn't and so, when United made him an offer, he joined up with the Tannadice club. That was in 1966 and his career there was to continue for almost twenty years with just an odd little hiatus when he went to Dumbarton for a short spell before going back to United and joining the coaching staff.

He recalls: 'It was Jerry Kerr who signed me for Dundee United. He was the manager then and it was the only real signing offer I had. The English clubs had me down for training and they talked about making offers – but the concrete offer came from United and I took it. Of course, I'd dreamed about Rangers coming in. When you went to Ibrox as a kid that was always going to be your dream. But I was realistic enough to

Walter Smith's first memory is of a Rangers-Queens Park game –
they met again last season in a Glasgow Cup game. Here striker
Bobby Williamson shoots for goal in Rangers' 2–1 victory

know that they weren't going to come for me and honest enough with myself to realise that I wanted to be a professional footballer and Dundee United were giving me that opportunity. It was six or seven years later that Jim McLean, who had been coach at Dundee, crossed the street to become the United manager.'

That was an important turning point in Smith's life. McLean, an influential coach, was a major factor in Smith's growing awareness of the coaching side of the game. Walter admits now: 'I always thought about the game and was interested in the tactical side of it. Even when I was a young player at Tannadice, say, still in my early twenties, I had ideas about the coaching side of things. When Jim McLean came to Tannadice he encouraged that in all the players. He wanted you to think about the tactical aspects of the game. Certainly if I'm ever asked who has influenced and helped me most then I would never go past him.

'He encouraged me to go to coaching courses, he gave me a job on the coaching staff at Tannadice and I learned a whole lot from him about the game. In a strange kind of way, you know, there is a strong Ibrox connection as regards Jim's own views on the game. He worked for a long time with John Prentice who played for Rangers and was a very under-rated manager with Clyde, with Scotland and with Dundee. In a way I reckon he is Jim's guru. They are still very close and John Prentice comes to games that United are playing in; he and Jim talk a lot together about how matches might be approached and all the rest. I think that Jim picked up some of his ideas from John Prentice. He then added his own tremendous knowledge and that mix was passed on to me and to others at Tannadice. Now I have the chance to bring the Prentice ideas back to Ibrox where he probably first developed them.'

It was at Tannadice Jim McLean gave Smith responsibility, and that led directly to his involvement with the Scotland set-up. He started off with the Under-18 youth squad, graduated to the Under-21 team and then, finally, to the full Scotland set-up where he was right-hand man to Alex Ferguson in Mexico. Says Smith: 'I owe a lot to Andy Roxburgh, the SFA chief coach, for getting involved with the Scots international set-up. He invited me to join him with the Under-18 side and that was tremendous experience for me.

More to stir Walter Smith's memory of his first ever time on the Ibrox terracings – Queens Park under pressure from Ally McCoist, who was a Smith protegé at Under-18 level for Scotland

'Then, presumably because of my job there and the job I had with Dundee United, the late Jock Stein promoted me to handling the Under-21 side. Then after Jock's death I went with Alex Ferguson.

'It is a very satisfying job to be with a national side at any level. I liked it with the Under-18's because there you had the chance to see the lads develop. They came to you with their skills but were still learning about the game. Some smashing players passed through the ranks of the Under-18 sides while I was involved.

'Charlie Nicholas played for the team, so did Paul McStay, and Ally McCoist who is with me again here at Ibrox. Then being with the Under-21 side you saw the lads again at another stage in their development. And finally you see them at the top, in the full international side, playing at World Cup level. It's a very satisfying thing to see them growing up so to speak. From youngsters just out of school to fully fledged professionals. It's good to see it.'

But it was not only his role with Scotland which persuaded David Holmes, the Ibrox chief executive, or Graeme Souness himself, that Walter Smith was his ideal running mate in the restructured backroom team at Ibrox. It was also his considerable achievements along with Jim McLean at Tannadice. Smith helped McLean guide the team to a championship win, to two League Cup victories and to several notable runs in Europe. The last carried these proud provincials to the semi-final of the European Cup – and to the brink of the Final itself. Ironically, looking back now, Smith and Souness would have been on opposite sides that year in the Final of the tournament in Rome!

But United failed to qualify by just a single goal in controversial circumstances against the Italian side Roma. Bribery allegations were made against the Roma president and the Italian FA eventually ordered a probe into whether or not the referee in the second leg had been bribed.

On merit United, with little or no resources compared to their much more powerful opponents, deserved a place in the Final against Liverpool. They had shown talent and discipline right through their run in the most prestigious tournament of all.

Remembers Smith: 'We really did play well that season. Possibly that year and the year before when we won the title were the peak years of my time with Dundee United. We were playing superb football and we should have beaten Roma over the two legs. It still seems incredible that we, as such a small team, were able to compete at that level, against the kind of teams we were being asked to meet. In the second round that year we destroyed Standard Liège of Belgium. Our performance over the two legs

Opposite: Top scorer Ally McCoist displays a style which leaves defenders flat-footed and gives goalkeepers nightmares

Above left: Nice one, son! Hibs are the victims this time and Doug Bell can't help smiling at the antics of his delighted team-mates
Above right: Ted McMinn, Rangers' big money buy from Queen of the South in 1984, invites the opposition to try to take the ball off him
Below: Dave McKinnon released at the end of last season, certainly doesn't lack aggression and determination as this action shot clearly shows

Spanish side Real Osasuna ended Rangers' UEFA Cup hopes in
October last year. But Craig Paterson still managed to make them
sweat

Hugh Burns being pursued by Celtic's Murdo MacLeod and Danny
McGrain as the action hots up in an Old Firm clash

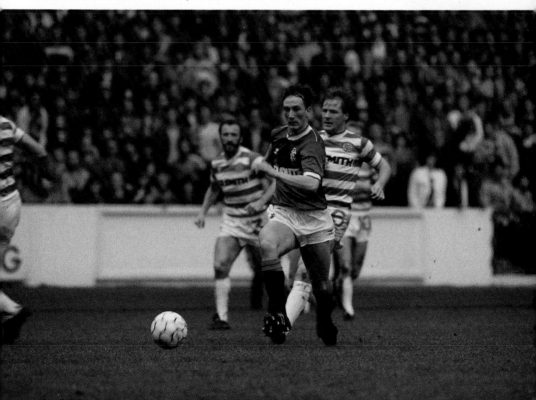

Above: Take that! Clyde on the receiving end of a 5-0 Skol Cup defeat and that man McCoist does it again

Below: The look on Ted McMinn's face says, 'It's my ball,' as the Motherwell defence race to cover

Opposite: I'm in charge! Dave McPherson mops up at the back and then prepares to set his forwards in motion

Above left: Oops! Stuart Munro experiences a few problems trying to control a bouncing ball

Above right: They shall not pass! Big Dave McPherson in commanding action against Motherwell.

Below: You can't stop me! Celtic's Peter Grant tries his best but Davie Cooper's silky skills leave his Old Firm rival in his wake

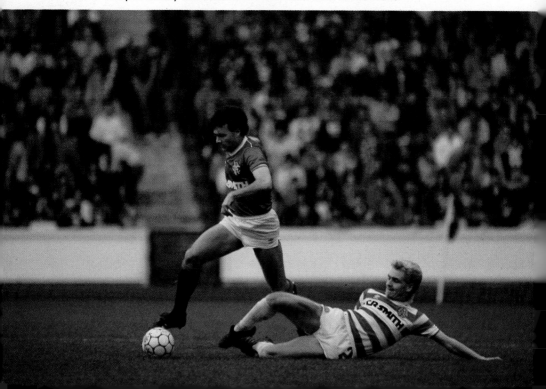

Bobby Williamson, one of the players who left Ibrox in the summer and joined West Bromwich Albion in a swap deal for Jimmy Nicholl

Ally McCoist bursts through despite the attention of the Motherwell defence and another of the 40 plus goals he scored last season is on the cards .

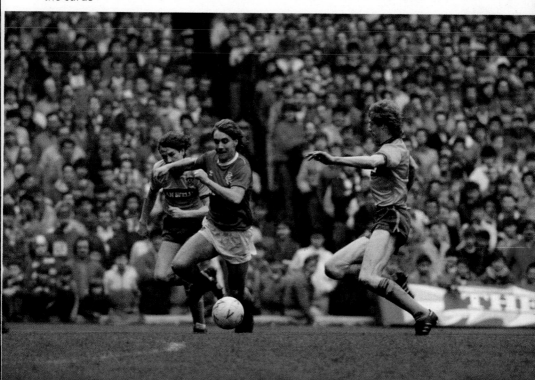

is possibly the best I can remember from my years with the club. We went over to Liège and didn't give them a shot at goal in the first leg. Then we brought them back to Tannadice and hammered four goals past them. The football we played was magnificent. In the quarter-final we beat Rapid Vienna – that was tighter. We lost 2–1 in Vienna and then won 1–0 at Tannadice so the away goal took us into the last four.

'It is still unbelievable that United could go into that last four. Alongside us were Liverpool, Dynamo Bucharest from Rumania and the team we were drawn against, the Italian champions Roma. Now Roma had the Brazilian stars Robert Falcao and Cerezo, as well as Italian internationals like Conti and Graziani. Yet we beat them 2–0 at Tannadice – and it could have been more on the night! Then came the second game with seventy thousand fans baying for our blood and we lost 3–0. It was a bitter disappointment for us. Yet it was a remarkable run for the club. There were good players in the side, intelligent players such as Paul Sturrock and Eamonn Bannon who went out there and never did less than a very good job for the team. Their attitude was superb all the time.

'But if we had been able to go out then and buy a quality midfield player, a really classy play-maker then I think United would have gone on to take the title again the following season. But we couldn't do it. The financial resources weren't there to allow us to really splash out. I know that Jim wanted to do that – but with a small club you have to trim your sails. You just cannot go out and do exactly what you want. You have to keep an eye on the money that you are spending because at a small club you just don't have the kind of financial clout that a club like Rangers has. That brings its own frustrations and it's always been a miracle to me that Jim McLean has been able to field such a successful side year after year, always able to compete with and match clubs who are much more powerful in terms of cash and support than United can ever hope to be.'

The European experience has helped Smith in his own approach to the game. He has looked at opposition sides from West Germany, from France, from Belgium and from Italy, from Yugoslavia and from Austria and he has picked up vital pieces of information. Now that knowledge, allied to the unrivalled experience of Souness on the field with Liverpool as they won European Cup after European Cup, will be directed towards helping Rangers overcome the European jinx which has dogged them remorselessly over the past seven or eight seasons.

Smith realises how important Europe is and he stresses: 'Our aim with Rangers has to be success on the Continent as well as success at home. Our fans want that – they demand that – and

Opposite: Coop in majestic action. The Ibrox World Cup winger shows the opposition a clean pair of heels

Graeme and I would love to give it to them. I think the fact that we have both been over the course so many times before will help us prepare the team. It takes time, all of this takes time, but we won't fall into too many of the obvious pitfalls.

'In a sense I've made my mistakes before probably just as Graeme has done. You go into the European thing at first and you change your team's tactics around, you ask players sometimes to do things that don't come naturally to them. I've seen other coaches and managers do it too. Then, you gradually realise that what you have to do all the time is play to your own strengths and be patient. There is not the slightest bit of use in going hell for leather in any of these European ties. Teams just sit back and wait for you, and if you lose your discipline then you lose the game. You always have to be sensible in your approach.

'Both Graeme and I know that the Rangers have to be in Europe every season. There is no way that we will drop our sights as regards that. If you are to make a reputation for the team then it has to be done in the real heat of European competition. Coming here at the end of last season I recognised the pressures which were on the club. We had to get into Europe and yet Dundee almost pipped us.

'Neither Graeme nor I expected to walk in and wave a couple of magic wands and find everything working out for us. That's why there was a lot of pressure over the last three matches. We lost the first – or at least, I lost the first because Graeme was still in Italy – then we got a very good draw up at Pittodrie. That was a really important result for us to get and the team played well that night. Then it was the Motherwell match and we knew that we had to win. If we won then we were in – if not, and if Dundee won, then we were out. It was a hard thing to contemplate. Rangers simply have to be in Europe. The revenue that a run in Europe engenders for a club as big as Rangers makes that vital. Dundee United could go into some of their European ties and lose money. You'd face terrible journeys to the wilds of Yugoslavia or somewhere else behind the Iron Curtain and the expense involved in that would eat away any cash raised from the first leg.

'That isn't the case with Rangers. A good, long run in one of the Continental competitions can raise the kind of money that any ambitious club needs. Graeme and I are aware of that. When we took on the two jobs we were told that money was available to buy players, top quality players. The club made that cash available to us but we recognise the fact that we cannot go on and on asking for cash without being able to produce some of it ourselves. Any major profits will be ploughed back into the club in any case to make sure that we can compete at the very highest level. So it's in everyone's interests to have success in Europe.

'It's in the interests of the club because it's there that the real excitement happens . . . .

'It's in the interests of the players because you become better players when you are competing regularly at that level. . . .

'It's in the interests of Graeme and I because both of us have

Yet another Ibrox player Walter Smith knows from his international role – right back Hugh Burns, who was with the Ibrox new man in the Scotland Under-21 team

One more familiar face from the Under-21 side – the tall Rangers sweeper Dave McPherson

ambitions for this club and they don't stop within the borders of Scotland . . . .

'And it's in the interests of the fans because they haven't changed down through the years. The big European nights are still those that appeal most of all. I don't believe for one moment that the Rangers support has changed from the days I used to go along to watch Fiorentina or Inter Milan. They're the kind of games they want to see.'

While recognising the critical importance of Europe, Smith also knows that the fans want to see a championship flag flying over the Ibrox Stadium. But, like Souness, there are no rash promises. He realises that the Premier League is a difficult League in which to succeed. The challenge from the top teams has intensified over the past half-dozen years and there are few signs that that challenge will fade away. Aberdeen, Dundee United, Hearts and Old Firm rivals Celtic, who won the title last season, will still be as powerful over the next season or two as the Rangers build-up progresses.

Admits Smith: 'There is a lot of work to be done and we are trying to get it done so that we can be challenging for honours after a year and then maybe looking to consolidate on that in another year. Nothing happens overnight in this game. We are overhauling the scouting system, setting up coaching classes for the school-age youngsters we will be trying to sign and stepping up our recruitment of these young players. Too many of them are being snapped up by other clubs. We don't want that to continue. We want to get our share – in fact we want more than our share because this is the biggest club in the country!

'People will be aware of what we are trying to do and that will help us when we are trying to sign young lads from school. The mere fact that Graeme is here will help us too. I think everyone would agree that Scotland's World Cup skipper carries a bit of clout!

'Working with Graeme is great. I got to know him on the run-in to Mexico and I realised immediately just how influential a player he is on the park. He provides leadership and that is essential in any side. He is not afraid of responsibility either and he has such tremendous vision and fantastic passing ability. The whole thing is a joy for me.

'I suppose the bonus is being where I always wanted to be – at Ibrox! And also being here under my own steam if you like. I was really disappointed the last time when the deal fell through with Jim McLean. But I knew then that I was only getting the job because of Jim. He wanted me – Rangers were just taking me as a part of his deal. This time I was wanted for my own sake. It was a recognition, if you like, of what I've been able to do for myself in the game. That was important to me.'

There will be a change of style with Rangers. Some of the more modern fluent game will gradually find its way into the tactics over the months ahead. Some of the changes have been noted already. Others will come. Souness will have his Liverpool background to draw upon. Smith will add his own Dundee United and Scotland knowledge to make the package work. It is a partnership which could bring back the glory years for Rangers. Smith, as Souness is first to stress, will be a vital ingredient. It has taken him thirty-three years to graduate from a place on the terracing with his grandfather to an office at the top of the impressive marble staircase. He has worked hard to get there – but getting the job he cherished hasn't changed him.

'Just being here at Ibrox is reward enough for anyone,' he grins, 'but for me there's the thought that I could also get the freedom of my father's bowling club! They're all Rangers supporters out there, you know.'

I DIDN'T THINK I'D EVER PLAY WITH GRAEME SOUNESS by Iain Durrant

The day that the former manager of the club left, that Monday at the start of April when all the changes took place, we had a reserve game at Ibrox. Going to the game that night no-one had the slightest clue about what was going on. Not one of the players knew of the drama which was being acted out upstairs in the boardroom or the manager's office. It was afterwards that the news filtered through to the dressing rooms.

Rumours had grown late in the afternoon about Jock Wallace leaving and then, also, that Graeme Souness was to take over. So at the end of that game, as you would imagine, there was little time to talk about anything else at all. None of us could believe it. It was like total disbelief at first and then we realised that something really big was happening at the club.

But Graeme Souness as player-manager? It just didn't seem possible. As a midfield player myself he had always been someone I admired. Someone I looked up to. The thought of actually playing alongside him was like a dream come true. The thought that I would get the chance to learn from him was just as exciting. I think all of us were stunned by the whole business. But I remember Derek Johnstone, one of the older players in the team that night, saying to us: 'This will be a great opportunity for the young players here. You're getting the chance to play alongside one of the really great players. It can only help all of you . . .'

That stuck with me over the next few weeks as we came to grips with the fact that the Scotland captain was to be both our gaffer and our playing partner on the field. I mean, I used to watch him on the telly and marvel at the way he could control games. Either with Liverpool in the English First Division, or in some of their important European Cup ties, or with Scotland as he captained them in their World Cup games.

Young Iain Durrant is under pressure here as Hibs' Gordon Chisholm tries to force him off the ball

Not once did I think that the opportunity to play with him would present itself. And it's only when you do actually play with him, or against him, that you realise the real measure of his greatness and his ability. The day after his appointment was more or less confirmed he came down to meet the players in the dressing room. Then in the following weeks he was at the training and he took part in a few practice matches with the rest of us.

That's when I knew that all the admiration I had for the Gaffer down through the years with Liverpool had been right. Trying to get near him when he is playing in opposition to you is a task and a half. It's at times like these when you begin to cotton on to the amount of work which is ahead of you as a young player. I think I'm being honest when I say that I am always ready to work at the game, that I'm always ready to listen, or to watch, and try to learn. On the field, though, is where you really learn your trade. And playing with men like the Gaffer is what helps most of all. They can teach you how to do the simplest but the most effective things. Everything the Gaffer does looks easy. It isn't, of course. You pick up on that very, very quickly when you see him at work in a practice game at the Albion!

I remember one of these games when I went to tackle him. I was sure that this time it was going to be my ball. In I went and, honestly, it was as if I didn't exist. He kind of shrugged me aside, moved away from me and then passed a perfect ball forward to one of his own players. I just stood there and watched him. I still don't know how he did it – but I was left stranded. And I mean really stranded! Some day I hope that I'll be able to learn just how to do that kind of thing. It's as Derek Johnstone said in the dressing room – this is the chance of a further education for the young players. I want to watch and listen and learn every minute we are at training.

The great thing, too, is that it's not just the Gaffer that you pick up from. The assistant manager Walter Smith is there too. He brought a fresh approach to the training routines inside the first couple of weeks he was there at the end of last season. In a short space of time he had altered everything. Where it seemed before that everyone was working on their own, Walter suddenly had everyone working as a team.

In the past the defenders had worked together, the midfield had worked together and the forwards had worked together. Walter Smith had us all moving together establishing links between each area – and none of the training sessions was ever in any danger of being boring. It was fresh and new to us and

Just too late – Durrant's expression says it all as he watches,
disappointedly, as St Mirren striker Frank McGarvey manages a shot
at goal. Durrant had just failed to make his challenge in time

Left: Former Aberdeen midfield man Dougie Bell, one of Durrant's rivals for a midfield spot last season

Right: Veteran Derek Johnstone, freed at the end of last season – he said in the dressing room how important the Souness appointment would be for the young players at Ibrox

I think that every player was like me – delighted to be a part of things!

The other good thing in these early days was that we realised very quickly what was wanted from us. There was no way that any of the fancy coaching jargon was going to be used.

What we heard was straight talking, solid sound, common sense. Everything was spelled out in simple football terms and all of us appreciated what was going on. We all felt that we wanted to respond, that we wanted to make sure after all the failures earlier in the season that Rangers would qualify for Europe. In the first match under Walter we failed. The team lost at Paisley to St Mirren and things moved in Dundee's direction as far as the one remaining place in Europe was concerned.

All of us knew what it would mean if we didn't get that place and we all felt kind of responsible for Rangers being in that position. We all had to lift ourselves and try to show the new bosses that we were ready to respond to the new régime. We went up to Pittodrie and drew, and then we just needed a win over Motherwell to finish off the season and to make certain that the UEFA Cup place would be clinched.

It looked simple enough on paper. There were Motherwell at the bottom of the League and we had beaten them twice before during the season. But the last match had ended with them winning 1–0 and they were intent on ending the season on a good note. They had made it hard for us, too, in the other games we had managed to win. We knew that it would not be easy and we all felt that Dundee would get something in their game against Hearts. I don't suppose we expected the upset there at Dens Park to be as big as it turned out to be, but we did know that Dundee had been playing well and were desperately keen to get that European spot for themselves.

Their manager, Archie Knox, had made no secret of the fact that this was his ambition – to lead the team into Europe. He knew, too, what playing in Europe was like from his days with Alex Ferguson at Aberdeen. Clearly Knox was missing the involvement at that level – and he wanted to be back amongst it all. Later, of course, he returned to Aberdeen during the close-season.

Just as clearly it was going to be a disaster for us if we could not get into the UEFA Cup. I reckon there was more pressure on us that day than at any other time during the season. But there was one thing to help us through – the reaction of the Ibrox support to the arrival for the first time of the new manager. The Gaffer could not play in the game but he was there, and before the match he and Walter Smith took their bows. There were more than twenty-one thousand people in the ground. More than there were at Paisley where Celtic were to win the League later that afternoon. And more than there were at Dens Park where fifteen thousand Hearts fans had travelled expecting to see their heroes take the title – only to have to watch in agony as Dundee beat them 2–0. Yet for our game, with all at stake being a place in Europe, and the opposition, with all due respect to Motherwell, being from the bottom of the Premier League, we outdrew the others.

I think that must have underlined to the new Boss what he had believed all along – that Rangers were the biggest club in

One of the big disappointments for Rangers and Durrant last season was defeat in this Tynecastle Cup tie. Durrant scored but Rangers lost 3–2 and crashed out of the Scottish Cup. Here is Hearts' first goal from ex-Rangers player Colin McAdam, turning away from goal with his arm raised in salute

the country! If there were any lingering doubts then they were laid to rest less than a week later. We had the Glasgow Cup Final to play against Celtic at Ibrox. They were coming as champions. We were there as also rans – but in an Old Firm game no-one can ever be written off. Earlier in the season in the 3–0 win over Celtic in the Premier League clash at Ibrox, I had scored a goal and it remains the most memorable game in my short career. Now, after losing at Celtic Park and drawing 4–4 in the last of the League meetings between the clubs we were asked to face each other again.

The Glasgow Cup in modern times is a fairly meaningless trophy. It doesn't allow the winners to qualify for Europe. The fixtures are fitted in just where it is possible to get a game played with the minimum of fuss and as little re-arrangement of the more important matches as possible. Mostly clubs look on the tournament nowadays as a chore, a set of fixtures which have to be fulfilled – but little more than that. Except when the Old Firm meet. Then it can be imbued with all the fervour of a major soccer event if the time is right. This time it was right.

Neither of us were in the Scottish Cup Final which was to be played at Hampden the next day between Hearts and Aberdeen. This was our consolation – and with Celtic as the newly crowned champions it was our turn to take them down a peg or two. It was also the first time for our new backroom staff to be in charge for an Old Firm match. Celtic wanted to confirm their superiority as champions and they wanted to give our new manager a defeat. Our support wanted a victory. Incredibly more than forty thousand fans appeared at Ibrox that night – and we won the game 3–2 after extra time. It was a night for Ally McCoist to remember. He scored a hat trick as the champions plunged to defeat and he helped Graeme Souness to his first trophy win as manager of Rangers!

After all the years of holding aloft that giant European Cup with Liverpool it might have been small beer for the Boss. But the crowd made sure that he knew the intensity of the rivalry between the two Glasgow clubs. He had experienced the Merseyside derby games between Everton and his own club Liverpool – but I would doubt if anything can match the fervour of an Old Firm clash. Whether it's in the Glasgow Cup, or anything else, there is a tension in the air which is like no other. I've felt it a few times now and I love it and the other players, the more experienced players, insist that even in a major European tie it's hard to get anything to compare with it.

Mind you, even though we did lose in Spain last season to Real Osasuna I did enjoy my first competitive match in Europe. It is a different kind of game that you have to play there and that first time for me we obviously played it the wrong way. We lost two goals in the first half and that is suicide in any European match. It's especially suicidal when you are trying to defend a one-goal lead. I felt that we were trying to play the game too fast, instead of sitting in and consolidating – but it was my first game and I didn't know enough about it to express any great opinions.

Now, though, I feel that the background that the new men at the top have will help us in Europe. It may take time as everyone says but I have the feeling that things are going to work out properly. If you examine the pedigree of the two new men then you know that Europe has been their second home over the past few years. Graeme Souness has won European Cups with Liverpool and, as well as that, has played in maybe fifty or sixty European ties. Walter Smith has been in charge of Dundee United for maybe around the same number of games in Europe. So what we have, what we are going to benefit from, is the experience of around one hundred competitive European matches between them. The experience is going to be invaluable for all the players at the club – not just for the young players like myself. Even the more experienced lads are going to pick on this. Like I said earlier, I enjoyed my first taste of Europe but I would have enjoyed it much more if I had had the chance to start off on a winning note. I think that is important. To go out there and get a result would have made our season. Instead we lost that match and soon afterwards went out of the Skol Cup. There is almost a domino effect when you do lose an important game; it's as if other vital games are lined up at almost the same time and so if one goes then they all go.

Maybe it wasn't quite as bad as that – but it seemed to be at the time. And the worst thing of all was that we were a better team than the Spaniards. We should have beaten them over the two legs. The freak conditions helped keep them in the tie at Ibrox – and also prevented me making my European début in front of our own support. The manager was ready to play me until he saw the rain lashing down on the pitch and he left me out, saving me from the testing conditions which affected everyone else eventually.

In a way that was a disappointment but I understood the manager's viewpoint. He was trying to protect me from the dreadful weather, allowing me to make such an important first appearance in conditions which would suit my style of play a whole lot better. Knowing that he was protecting me helped me overcome my upset at being left out. Of course, the trouble was that when I did play for the first time in Europe it was in the second leg defeat – and nothing could help me get over that!

Still, when I think back just three years or so ago when I was still playing for Glasgow United in the juvenile leagues, it's really something to be talking about Europe now.

That's where I was spotted by Rangers and signed by them as a kid. Then I was called up by Jock Wallace in season 1984–85 as a full-time player. It was all I ever wanted to be. I was looked on then as a midfield player and that's where I have stayed and that's where I always prefer to play. On occasions with Glasgow United I pushed further forward and there were times when I played centre-forward or outside right. But everyone knew that I liked to play in the middle of the park, and I still do.

Maybe I try to go forward too much. But, with the Gaffer alongside me, perhaps I'll learn a little more about when I should make runs forward or when I might have to sit in a little. It's part of the learning I'll be doing over the next season or

A defeat from St Mirren and all the dejection of a season going wrong is mirrored in the look of defender Dave McKinnon

two and it's something I'm looking forward to. I know within myself that I could be a better player defensively. I reckon I could take up much better positions on the field when the other team gain possession. But while my strong point is going forward I think I could learn to be a better finisher as well. If I could brush up on both these parts of my game then I'd be happier. To be able to know the defensive roles that are important for a midfield man and ally that knowledge to better finishing would help make me a more complete player.

That has to be my aim – to be as good an all-round professional as possible. In the new set up I'm sure that is going to be possible. I'll be working as hard as I know how to make myself a better player and, with the help I'm sure is going to be around, then maybe I'll turn out as good a player as I want to be. If only I could finish a little better!

Let's hope that comes right and let's hope that future European games don't carry the same sad and disappointing messages for me. It would be so good to find success in Europe, for me, for Rangers and for the supporters. They helped make my season last time round and I feel I would like to help win something just for them. They deserve that just as much as any of the players do!

MY AMBITIONS - MORE CAPS AND A TITLE
by Ally McCoist

I had my best ever scoring season last year with Rangers –
thirty-two goals for the club and that helped earn me my first
ever cap for my country. First the Scotland manager, Alex
Ferguson, picked me for a friendly against Israel in Tel Aviv,
but I could only make the subs bench.

Then, later in the season, in the last warm-up game before
the team flew out for Mexico I played against Holland in
Eindhoven. It was a tremendous experience, but I'm determined
that it won't be a one-off situation for me as far as my country
is concerned. Since turning senior, first of all with St Johnstone
and then with Sunderland before coming back to Rangers, I
have been capped at Under-18 level, at Under-21 level and now
I have that full cap. I want more to follow it. And maybe there
was a hint from Alex Ferguson that I have earned further
consideration when he telephoned me to tell me personally that
I wasn't going to be included in his pool of players from which
the World Cup twenty-two were to be selected.

He didn't have to do that. I hadn't played in any of the
qualifying games and I knew myself that I was in the Holland
match because other players were not available – players who
were ahead of me in the running for the Finals. Despite the
pressure from the Rangers fans to try to get the national team
manager to put me into the squad, I never really believed that
I had a claim for Mexico. But when he 'phoned me I felt, then,
that maybe there was hope for me after Mexico. I know the
team manager will change but if I did well enough in my first
game to impress Alex Ferguson, and if I can keep scoring goals
the way I did last season, then my hopes of more caps will stay
very much alive.

That first honour was a tremendous thing for me. Going over
to Holland I was looking at the rest of the squad, wondering
who would be playing against the Dutch, although I did feel
that I had a chance to make my début there. The night before
the game the manager told me I was playing and I felt great.
Nervous, excited, but, above all, just very satisfied that I was

to get my cap. Now I have that Scotland number nine jersey and no one can ever take that away from me!

Afterwards there was a bonus for me when Alex Ferguson came out and publicly said how pleased he had been with my performance. That was the icing on the cake as far as I was concerned.

The fact that I accepted I would not be going to Mexico meant that there was very little pressure on me. I knew that it would take a combination of things for me to edge into the

Derek Ferguson, one of the youngsters McCoist believes will improve under the tutelage of new boss Souness

squad for the Finals. There were too many strikers ahead of me in the plans and it would have taken a bundle of injuries and a whole lot of luck before I could find myself in the frame. So I didn't have too much to prove – I could go out to enjoy the game which is exactly what I did!

Actually, the other thing going for me that time was that the game was against Holland and if there is one country I like to play against then that's the one. I've been lucky enough to play in Holland quite a few times. At youth level and in club games and they have always been good opponents. Good footballers, skilful players and well organised at the same time. You rarely see one of their players looking uneasy with the ball at his feet. They all look confident and comfortable and I have the impression always that anyone in the team could change positions with one of his mates and still be able to do the job. For instance the defenders often look as skilful as the front men. It's an all-round ability they seem to be taught and I find it impressive. Mind you, they have the kind of facilities over there that we simply can't match. They have coaching centres which are out of this world. Every facility you need is there and young and experienced players alike are always able to use them to improve their knowledge and techniques. We don't have anything to compare at all, one reasonably good centre at Inverclyde, at Largs, and that is about it.

Anyhow, that's another matter. Back to the game against the Dutch which we drew 0–0. First of all when I went there and found myself in the team, I simply wanted to enjoy the experience. Knowing that Mexico was out of the question I was able to do that. So when things worked out for me it was fine. I suppose, at the back of my mind, there was the hope that I could do well enough to improve my chances for the future. But while that possibly happened it wasn't the major thing for me. I really wanted to get out there in that Scotland jersey and enjoy all that was happening around me.

Actually, before the game, because of the unavailability of so many of the English based players no-one gave us too much of a chance and that's not a bad position to be in. I think Scots players prefer to have things that way, rather than be expected to win a match. It's when we are being tipped for victory that things start to go terribly wrong. That night in Eindhoven no-one expected us to win, or even get the creditable draw that we came away with. No-one except the Boss and the players, that is. We felt reasonably confident in our own ability and I think we proved to people that the Premier League is underestimated.

I've played in the English First Division with Sunderland so

A tussle with veteran Celtic full back Danny McGrain in one of the
Old Firm games that McCoist enjoys so much

I feel that I'm qualified enough to talk about the two leagues. Quite honestly the top half-dozen teams in the Premier Division would be well able to hold their own in the English First Division. The teams here at home have good players, good organisation and are as fit as any teams in the south. If any of our own fans had doubts about that they had only to take a look at the match in Holland.

Robert Connor of Dundee was outstanding, and yet people were surprised when he was picked for the match. He looked classy and confident and I reckon he surprised the Dutch by the quality of his passing. I played up front with Paul Sturrock and, again, you are talking about playing with someone who is an absolute professional. He kept running at the Dutch defenders and they didn't know how to handle him. Twice he was brought down and twice we should have been given penalties. None of us know yet why we weren't. Then there was Maurice Malpas sitting in the midfield and playing with real authority – what a good player he is!

But it was a really solid team performance and with any luck at all we would have won the game. That was away from home against a strong Dutch team which had failed only in a play-off against their most deadly rivals Belgium to make the Mexican Finals.

Funnily enough, although I was stepping up to another higher level of the game I found that I had more time to play. More time on the ball, more time to make passes, more time to get in shots at goal. I've heard other players say this about international football and I found it was correct. It's nice for a forward – and, of course, I had Coop out on the left wing so it was just like being at Ibrox. You know what he is going to do with the crosses and all you have to do is try to get on the end of them. It was a big help to me having Davie there. I think that worked out well and having Paul Sturrock guiding me through it was another big help.

It was a lot different from the Premier League where you don't get any time at all, when defenders are breathing down your neck and biting into tackles whenever you try to gather a ball. It's a tough league for forwards to play in – but I suppose you reap the benefit of that when you get into a different environment and can revel in the time you are allowed, whether it's at international level or in the European competition matches. Even there, with the usual system of man-for-man marking it can still be a little bit easier on you than the game at home where, so often, everything seems to be done at a hundred miles an hour!

Ally leaves one-time Sunderland playing pal and an ex-Rangers player, Iain Munro, stranded as he gets in a shot in this clash with Hibs

There was just one disappointment for me – that the new manager Graeme Souness was ill and could not travel from Italy to play in the game. It was a let down that he wasn't there, not from the point of view of him being able to see me play for Scotland – but from the point of view of playing with him. I was looking forward to having that chance.

Joining up with the Boss at club level is something that everyone in the side looked forward to. Just his very presence there was special – but as well as his presence, there is his amazing ability. The young lads in midfield, Iain Durrant and Derek Ferguson, are going to come on a ton being in there beside him. Just watching what he does, how he plays and how he reacts to situations will be an education to them – and to all the rest of us. It is a whole new experience.

I scored those thirty-two goals last season, which was eight better than I'd ever done before. I once managed twenty-four when I was still with St Johnstone. Now I would like to go higher if I can, and with the Boss pushing the odd pass through to me then maybe there are chances. Plus, when I heard about my old Sunderland mate Colin West signing for us I knew that would be a benefit for me. I played with Westy at Roker Park and I enjoyed it there. He's always been the kind of player I enjoy playing with. Big, strong, good in the air, able to get goals himself and able to help people around about him get goals too. If I could get into the same scoring groove as I was in last season then maybe I can help Rangers win a title. I think I would like that more than anything else. Even more games for Scotland is lower on my list of priorities than that. The club has been crying out for success since I came back. I know we have had a couple of League Cups to placate the support, but that's not enough; the club want more than that and they deserve more than that.

We did give them the Glasgow Cup last season of course. Now I know that must seem a non-event to most people outside of Glasgow, but what a finale to the season it was for us – and for me especially. I grabbed a hat-trick against Celtic that night and it was the first Old Firm match when the new manager was in charge of the team. We all wanted to give him a winning start against Celtic and we were able to do it in extra-time with my third goal clinching a 3–2 win. That's not my first hat-trick in an Old Firm game, because I did it once before in the Skol Cup Final at Hampden when we beat them. I enjoy these games and I have a good record in them. Since joining up at Ibrox I have scored eleven goals in thirteen games against Celtic. I get a real kick out of scoring in one of these matches. In fact it

More action from a Hibs encounter as Scotland's top scoring Premier League striker Ally McCoist is tackled by Gordon Hunter in another Ibrox attack

Scotland and Rangers winger Davie Cooper – he helped McCoist in his international debut against Holland

brings me immense joy because the Old Firm game is the best 'derby' game in the world and getting a goal in that one really means something.

But while we were able to deliver the goods that night I know how upset all of the players were when our League challenge just died away after we had made our best start in seasons. It's

An unorthodox challenge from the grounded Hibs defender Gordon
Rae as he tries to thwart McCoist in the League Cup tie which
Rangers lost at Easter Road

Another of the teenage midfield men McCoist is convinced will benefit from playing alongside Souness – here is Iain Durrant on the ball

often been the case that Rangers begin badly, give the other teams a start and then are left trying to pull the others back when the League has gone beyond our reach. It was different this time. We had a good start with five wins out of six games and the other match was a 1–1 draw with Celtic at Parkhead. We were off and running – or so it seemed. And in the tightest race ever for the Premier League title, if we had been able to hang in there, then I'm sure we could have come desperately close to taking the flag. After all, the other teams involved began to cut each other's throats and that went on right until the last day of the season. I would have given anything to be involved in that. Instead while Celtic and Hearts were deciding where the flag ended up we were worrying over the last place in Europe! It wasn't good enough and I know all the lads would agree with that.

Our level of consistency dropped dramatically after that opening burst. After playing Osasuna in the first leg UEFA Cup game at Ibrox we went on a disaster run. We lost four games in a row – and suddenly we were struggling. We picked up a reasonable result or two after that but I think the damage had been done by then. We went out of Europe, slipped from the top of the table and lost two goals to Hibs in the Skol Cup first leg. We tried to come back in the second leg at Ibrox but although I scored that night it wasn't enough, so two of the tournaments we were in had gone – and the League was rapidly slipping away. I think some of our inexperience showed in that spell. We lost our way completely. There were suspensions which didn't help, and injuries, but basically it was down to ourselves as players not being able to reach the level of consistency which had kept us going so strongly in the early weeks of the season. In fact we never did get that back. And to win titles you must be able to string results together week after week after week. Look at the way Hearts did it to maintain their challenge to the end. And look how Celtic did the same as Liverpool and came in with a late run of successive wins which kept the pressure on the less experienced Hearts until eventually, on the last day, the Tynecastle men cracked under the strain. You must be able to remain consistent. If you don't then you can win a Cup but you will never win a title. And as I said earlier it's the title that we want to be able to give to the fans before very long.

Personally, I believe that the club is going places. My contract ended last summer and while I always wanted to stay at Ibrox because of what it means to me, I suppose I could have been tempted away. But when the changes at the top happened my mind was made up!

You know the effect that the signing of Graeme Souness as player-manager had right across the country. Well, inside Ibrox it was the same. It was as if a tornado had struck the place. There was a buzz around the dressing rooms, the whole of the stadium seemed to have been lifted by what had happened because none of us had ever believed that such a major signing was possible for the club.

I think it was a tremendously imaginative move and it's going to pay off handsomely for the club and for all of us as players. The partnership, on and off the park, of the manager and his assistant, Walter Smith, will be vital for us. I see it as an ideal situation. It's important having a leader on the field as well as having guidance off the park.

Aberdeen have Willie Miller as their leader, Celtic have big Roy Aitken – well now we have someone as well. Someone who has the kind of presence about him which makes opponents tread a little warily. Everyone knows that he is a class player – but I think too that he is a player who is influential. He can dictate the way that a game should go. The sheer presence of the man is unreal. There is never any doubt that Graeme Souness will get respect from everyone round about him – the players at Ibrox and the players from other clubs. And while we have all of that on the park with us as a little bonus, or rather a big, big bonus, we have him as manager off the park to provide guidance from that direction. And as his right-hand man there is Walter Smith, who is recognised throughout the country – and probably even in Europe – as one of the top coaches in the business.

I know Walter well because I played for the Under-18 team and again with the Under-21 team when he was coach. I don't think I know any coach who is more universally liked and respected by players than Wattie. You will never hear any of the lads say anything against him. He has tremendous knowledge and he has the ability to impart that knowledge to players. He manages to make the game sound so simple and all the time he is getting his message across to you. Having him allied to the Boss was a master stroke.

My only worry is that I once locked Wattie out on a balcony in Monte Carlo – I'm just hoping that he has forgiven me for that. Or even better forgotten all about it. We were there playing in a youth tournament in Monaco and Wattie was coming round to check the rooms one night and make sure all the lads were in bed. This was the Under-18 national squad, by the way. So when he came into my room and stepped out on the balcony to

Ally McCoist reckons the Premier League is tough on strikers – here's
evidence to back him up. Ted McMinn is sent crashing with a rugby
style tackle from Motherwell's Iain McLeod

Now McMinn reacts after being sent sprawling on the touchline, in
the kind of incident which occurs regularly in the dog-eat-dog
atmosphere of Scotland's top division

take a look at the swimming pool, I shut the door on him – and locked it!

Well, it was funny for a minute or two but when I saw that he was getting angry my bottle went. I mean, it really did. I thought, what have I done? He'll kill me – so I threw the key to someone else in the room and ran. I just got out of the room as fast as my legs would carry me. Retribution did catch me up, though. . . .

But these trips with the Under-18 team were good. You were learning your trade at a fairly high level and doing it in so many different countries and, again, that's an aspect of a player's development which is more important than people might realise. It's when you are playing against other countries that you learn different approaches to the game. And you pick up on how to combat playing against the 'sweeper' system which so many of the Continentals use, or against the man-for-man marking which can make it hard for strikers. I've been lucky because even at youth level I've been able to go to West Germany, Holland, Belgium, Iceland, France and Spain. And my education has continued with Sunderland and with Rangers. Not that Sunderland played in any of the European tournaments but they did take on tours and pre-season training games; that was when I realised how well-equipped the Dutch training centres were compared to what we have at home. We would stay in one of these centres and it was the best way to prepare for a new season at home. Everything you required was there. I like Holland. I like the football they play and their whole approach to the game – so it was good that I got my first cap there.

I know that I can't sit back and rest on any laurels I picked up in getting that cap and scoring those goals last season. I have to keep going, keep working at my game, keep trying to improve myself. It's the only way for me – or for anyone who wants to be a success. I don't mind the challenge for places that there is at Ibrox and that's something which might be intensified. That is something that keeps an edge to your game. I'm just happy that I'm still with the club when it seems ready to take off. I know from my signing talks that the ambitions are high. Just to be a part of that, a part of a really successful Rangers team, will be a tremendous boost for me. I have no doubts that things are going to happen at Ibrox – big things – the kind of things that any player wants to be a part of. I told Mr Holmes that when I signed. I want to stay with Rangers and especially now I know the direction they are moving in. This club is going UP – and I want to rise with it!

THE MAN AT THE TOP

Silvery-haired David Holmes is one of Britain's leading business executives as UK Managing Director of the massive multinational, multi-million pound John Lawrence empire . . .

He is also, more to the point as far as the people who follow Rangers are concerned, the chief executive of Rangers Football Club. And Holmes is the man who has master-minded the changes which the club hope will carry them back to the top. Not just at home in Scotland but in Europe.

Graeme Souness insists that Rangers are a side who should be linked in the minds of the soccer public with the European greats and Holmes agrees. In his office adjoining Ibrox he contemplates a bright future for a club which was struggling to keep up with the achievements of their rivals in Scotland's Premier League. Holmes wants better than that for the club. He has the same fierce ambition for Rangers as he does for the Lawrence group of companies. That is why he made the dramatic signing move for Souness, and why he linked the Scotland skipper with the Scotland coach Walter Smith, to form a management team which would fit into the backroom set-up he has devised.

Says Holmes: 'People keep telling me that you cannot use the same ideas in football as you do in business. I don't believe that. In a business you make it successful by getting the management team right. That's what we have done. I have the men to look after the team on the park; and off the field we have Campbell Ogilvie as club secretary, who will concentrate on the administration, and myself as chief executive. We then have the other members of the board who have various duties.

'After setting all of that up we had to get other aspects right as well. Marketing and selling are different things, you know, although most people don't realise that!

'Marketing means getting the product right, whatever that product may be. You have to have everything properly done so that you can make the hard sell. If you don't have the marketing right then you will be going into the market place with inferior

Rangers' Chief Executive David Holmes behind his desk – where he planned his Souness signing coup

goods. I think that is what was happening at Ibrox. We weren't giving our loyal supporters value for money. That had to change.'

It began to change when Lawrence Marlborough, the chief shareholder of the club decided to buy outright control of Rangers with Holmes acting as chief executive. There was criticism at the time, suggestions that Rangers had become a mere subsidiary of the building conglomerate. That in future the club would take a back seat to the other business interests of the group. That, though, was not what Marlborough wanted. Nor what Holmes intended.

Club secretary Campbell Ogilvie, the man who is in charge of administration in Holmes' new Ibrox backroom team

Holmes stresses: 'I have talked about the club being a subsidiary myself because in a business sense that is exactly what it is! You can't change that. But, where people get it wrong is in their attitude to that word "subsidiary". It does not mean that Rangers Football Club is to be downgraded or neglected. We have proved that by the way we have handled things in appointing Graeme as manager.

'But we also recognise how important the club is for the rest of the group. It can be a big earner, of course, if it is run on the right lines and is made a success. But we are not interested in the profits as such – we are interested in the prestige that the club can bring to the rest of the group. If we have something as high profile as a top European football team then we must cherish that.

'If the club makes money then that money will be ploughed back into the team. It will be used to help maintain the stadium or to buy players that the management team want. We made money available when Graeme and Walter took control and the one stipulation I made was that I did not want the money wasted. I wanted to have top quality players coming to Rangers and I knew that we would get them with Graeme having already set the trend. When we made the first signing of Colin West from Watford, Graeme didn't have any trouble convincing the lad that the club was big and that it had a great future stretching out in front of it – and that he could be a part of that future. OK, it was reversing a trend whereby players have gone south, but top players have rarely moved north from the English First Division. But we intend changing a whole lot of things.'

Holmes is there in the wings ready to give advice if that is required and ready to give hard cash when players are wanted. Other than that he will not interfere. When Souness decided to free long term Rangers Dave McKinnon and Derek Johnstone it was a decision made by him and Walter Smith. Holmes was not consulted.

The Ibrox overlord admits: 'I don't want to be consulted on the playing aspects. That is not my business. My job was to put the right men in charge and I believe that I have done that. I can tell you this – in my first meetings with both Graeme and Walter there was one thing which impressed me mightily about both of them as men. They were more interested in the job they were being offered than the money which might be available. All they talked about was the job and what they believed they might be able to achieve. They didn't start bickering over salaries. The job came first and foremost and I found that refreshing. Don't get me wrong, they will be well paid, but that was not their priority. The real charge for them lay in the job they were being offered and the ambitions that the club had. I spelled it out to both men.

'It's no longer enough to struggle along as Rangers have been doing. We must get success. We must get trophies here at home and we must re-establish the side in Europe. It's not enough to go into a Continental competition for the first or second round and then suddenly be out on your ear. That's not the way

Holmes, (*left*) with his new manager Graeme Souness and fellow director Freddy Fletcher

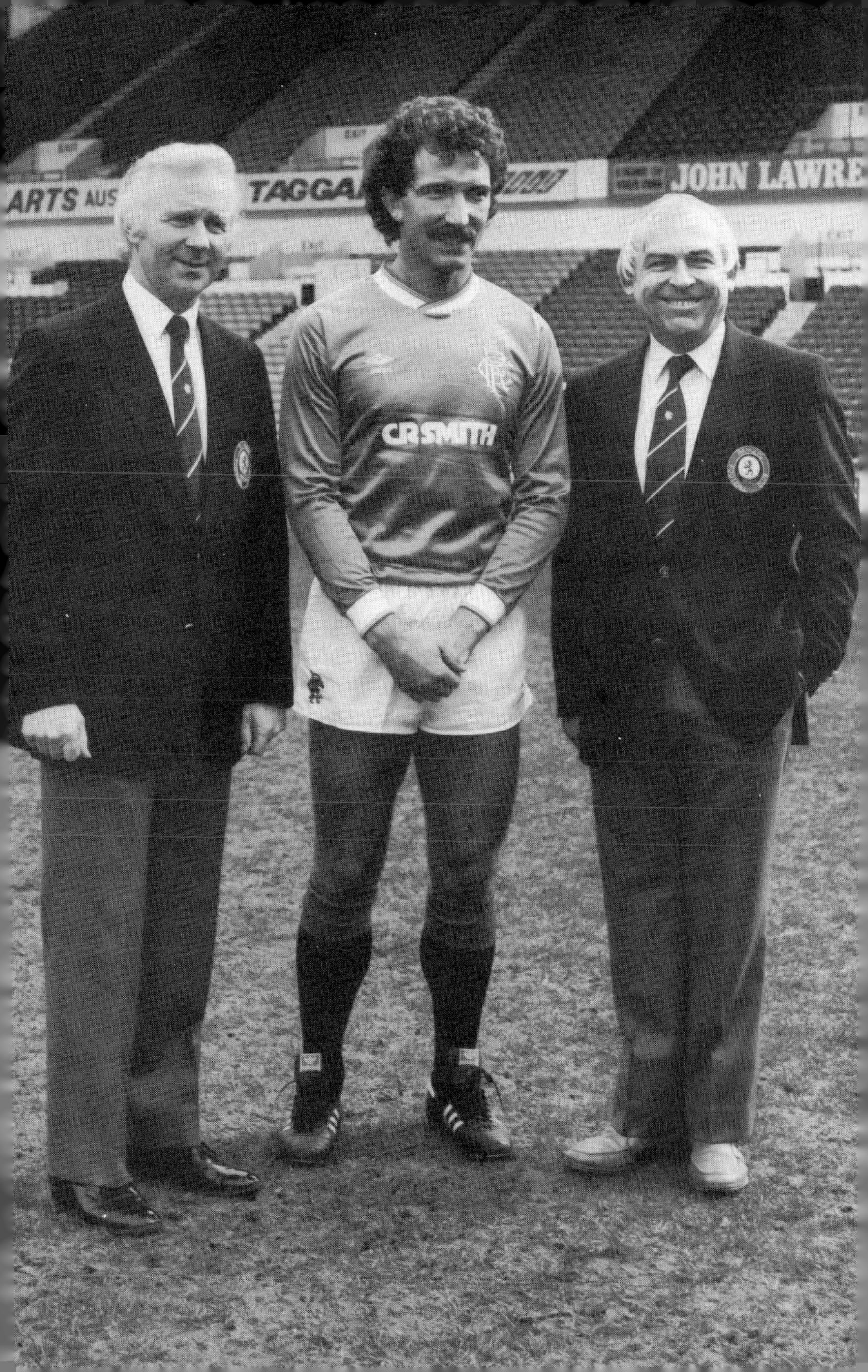
ARTS AUS
TAGGA
JOHN LAWRE
CRSMITH

Rangers were in their great days and it's not the way I want them to be now.

'I'm sure that I'm speaking for all the supporters when I say that. I'm very aware of what the support means to the club and we want to repay them for the loyalty they have given Rangers through some gloomy times. It has been amazing that they have kept coming along even when they knew the team was not getting any better.

'And there, at the end of the season, they were still turning up. Maybe with fresh hope because of the appointments we had made. Forty-one thousand people at a Glasgow Cup game – that's amazing and twenty-one thousand to see us play Motherwell in the last League game of the season!'

As well as these early indications of the impact the Souness appointment has made, Rangers were forced by public demand to place their season tickets on sale before the end of last season.

'We had a tremendous demand,' smiles Holmes, 'and it was an obvious spin-off from the announcement of the managerial

Veteran Derek Johnstone, freed by Souness in a move which Holmes did not know about. 'Decisions like that are left to Graeme and Walter Smith,' says the Ibrox supremo

The Ibrox Trophy Room – this is where Holmes wants to see the top prizes in the game

changes. The public wanted the season tickets on sale early and we had to bow to their demands. It was quite incredible but I think it helped show me that the decision to bring Graeme and Walter was the right one.

'When I first talked about Graeme Souness, because I had read that he was unsettled at Sampdoria, people pooh-poohed the thought. They didn't think I would succeed. But I'm a pretty determined man and if I want something badly enough I don't give up easily. I wanted Graeme because I'm a Souness fan and I thought he was right for Rangers. That's why I didn't rest until he was a Rangers man!'

That determination shook the soccer world. Not only in Scotland but south of the border and in Europe as well. There was one of the Continent's top stars, Scotland's World Cup captain, quitting an Italian First Division club to go home to Scotland. No one could grasp it. Particularly First Division supremos in England who had also tried to tempt Souness back to Britain. Spurs' millionaire chairman Irving Scholar for one, Chelsea's equally wealthy chairman Ken Bates for another; both were left at the post by the new man in football.

The one-time joiner and woodwork lecturer from Falkirk had beaten off the bigger guns. By doing so he had established an immediate reputation for himself. And with one stroke, with one imaginative coup, had placed Rangers firmly back on the map. It was a deal which was talked about in Italy and in Spain. In Holland and in West Germany. Indeed, everywhere football was played people sat up to take notice and wondered if the rebirth of Rangers was ready to take place. . . .

Holmes has few doubts that it will happen. He says: 'We had to act quickly and we had to act dramatically. It was no use going along the road we were going. I have great respect for Jock Wallace and the achievements he had with this club. But it was time for change, time for new faces, time for fresh ideas. That's why the whole backroom staff had to go with Jock. We couldn't continue with them. We wanted a new team and we wanted the best team available to us. I think we have that.

'Results will prove whether I'm right or not. But when you get men who are used to success and who still want more then you are going in the right direction. It is not something that happens overnight. Hard work has to go into it. Planning has to be done. Forward thinking is essential – but we will do all of that and then we will not sit back and hope results will follow. We will keep working and keep building to ensure that if we get success then we will keep success.

'Rangers are a big, big club. An institution if you like – but we have to have that institution modernised and streamlined. I know how Graeme and Walter are approaching the job and watching them simply makes me more and more delighted that they agreed to come here. If you set your sights high enough then things can come right for you. With Rangers it would be a mistake to lower your sights. To do that means lowering your ambitions which also means lowering your standards. That won't be happening any more. We want the best and nothing but the best!'

Like other Rangers people Holmes was concerned at the absence of any major Rangers presence in the Scotland World Cup set-up. Winger Davie Cooper was the one man who was a regular. In one signing swoop Holmes altered that. Souness and Smith went to Mexico as important members of the Scotland squad – and suddenly Rangers were again where they should be in the international scene.

Explained Holmes: 'When I was younger the Scotland team always had Rangers players. Not just one or two but quite a

Davie Cooper, until the arrival of Souness, the one regular from
Rangers in the Scotland squad – and this is just one of the ways
used to stop the wing ace!

few. We want to get back to those days by having the quality
players here that Scotland will select. If you look down through
the years you can remember George Young, Eric Caldow and
John Greig who all captained their country regularly. Now we
have Graeme doing that and we have Ally McCoist knocking
at the door. That's the way we would like it to be.

'I think it's important for all of us that Scotland do well –
and if Rangers can help them, that will be a bonus for all of us
at Ibrox.'

Inside six months of becoming a Rangers director David
Holmes turned the staid, often old fashioned world of Scottish
soccer on its head. I have the feeling that he enjoyed doing it –

and he will not rest until Rangers are back where he believes they belong. If he has to produce more rabbits from hats then I'm sure that will be done.

Holmes wants things right. After his initial flurry I'm convinced that he will get them right. His backroom shuffle was both ambitious and sound. His negotiations to keep Ally McCoist at Ibrox were bold and big. No-one will leave Ibrox again because they can better themselves elsewhere. I doubt if Holmes would allow that.

He wants Rangers to be big and he has the thinking to match these dreams.

Ally McCoist, the scoring star who was given the terms that Rangers' top players will now enjoy under the new régime

MY BEST MOVE
by Colin West

Colin West, Rangers' close-season signing from Watford, declared himself an Ibrox fan within minutes of his arrival at the stadium in May.

Looking almost overawed, the quiet-spoken Englishman faced the Scottish press for the first time and admitted: 'I had heard that Ibrox was something special but I didn't bargain for this. It must be one of the finest soccer stadiums in the world.'

West's arrival as manager Graeme Souness's first signing came as something of a surprise. But it was at least a pleasant one for fellow striker Ally McCoist. The pair played together at Sunderland and it was a partnership which both believed should have been given greater scope at the time.

Striker Ally McCoist, an old Roker Park mate of Colin West's, in a clash with another ex-Sunderland man, Gordon Chisholm of Hibs

When McCoist left Roker Park to join Rangers, and West eventually moved on to Watford, it seemed highly unlikely that they would ever be given the chance to become a double-act, especially in the Premier League.

But manager Souness clearly saw the potential in the pairing and it didn't require very much persuasion on the part of the new boss to convince the 24-year-old, 6 feet 2 inch, 13½ stone goal-scorer to take his talents north.

West takes up the story of the deal: 'When Graeme Souness first approached me about joining Rangers it came as a big surprise. But I didn't need time to think over the move. Rangers' reputation as a top club is known to everyone in the game.

'Apart from that aspect, Graeme Souness is a man I have always admired. He has an aura about him and when I met him at Gatwick airport he didn't need to employ any special powers of persuasion.

'He simply told me that he believed I could do a good job for Rangers and there was the added bonus of playing in Europe – a thrill I had not experienced before either at Sunderland or Watford.

'Despite being born in the north east I have no Scottish connections. But I had heard a lot about Rangers and Glasgow from Ally McCoist and John McClelland, who was a team-mate at Watford.

'So I was delighted to sign a three-year contract – I would have been happy to sign on for longer. However, I'll have to prove myself worthy of that.'

Like Graeme Souness before him, West might have been one of the stars of White Hart Lane but for a hankering to return home as a teenager and try his luck elsewhere.

'I spent six weeks with Spurs,' he says, 'but I didn't fancy it all that much. I suppose I suffered from a touch of homesickness and decided to try for a career elsewhere.

'I was just a kid at the time and London is a bit different from Wallsend, where I was born. It can be a very impersonal city and a shade overpowering for a youngster away from home for the first time.'

Almost inevitably several other clubs took an interest in West, who was more used to playing centre-half or midfield at the time.

Having played for his school team in North Shields and won representative honours at county level, it was natural that young

Heads, who wins? West and a Chelsea rival, Joe McLaughlin, fight it out in an aerial duel for the ball

Left: Looking good – Colin West is poised to unleash another powerful drive for Watford

Right: Colin West displays all his strength and power as he moves in to threaten danger and keep the Watford fans happy

West should come to the attention of local side Sunderland. And at the age of 14 he began training at Roker Park where he was to spend almost the next seven years carving out a career in football.

Looking back, West says: 'I enjoyed my career with Sunderland. They are a big club in many ways and the fans up there are as partisan as any in the country.

'In all, I played more than 100 first team games for Sunderland including a few with Ally McCoist in the side. I also had experience of playing against the best sides in England at places like Anfield, Goodison, Old Trafford and Highbury.'

But it wasn't all sweetness and light for West. When the end came for him at Sunderland it did so in rather unpleasant circumstances.

Having played a key role in helping take Sunderland to Wembley for the 1985 Milk Cup Final against Norwich, West was eagerly looking forward to a place on one of football's biggest stages.

Then the blow fell – and the striker found his Wembley dream had turned into a nightmare that few would have anticipated.

He takes up the story: 'I had played in every one of our Milk Cup-ties including the two semi-final matches with Chelsea. I had also scored twice against them and felt I had played well.

'You can imagine my feelings when the manager took me aside and told me I wouldn't be playing in the final. He explained that he wanted to play a sweeper at the back and there wasn't a place for me in the formation.

'It was a tremendous blow and I was naturally bitterly disappointed. The fact that Sunderland lost 1–0 didn't give me any satisfaction or make up for missing out on such a special occasion.

'I felt that it was time for me to be on my way from Roker. I had a talk with the boss, then Len Ashurst, and it was eventually decided that I should join Watford in a transfer deal that was valued at something like £100,000.

'Despite what had happened I was sorry to leave Sunderland because I had a lot of good times there. But the move to Watford turned out to be good for me.

'They are a friendly club and a well organised side. Everyone, from the youngest apprentice right up to the chairman, Elton John, takes an active interest in what's happening.

'I also managed to get among the goals, hitting 16 in 43 matches, and ended up top scorer. Seven of them came in our last 12 matches so I suppose that made people sit up and take a bit more notice of my play.

'Certainly, had Rangers not come in for me I would have been quite happy to remain a Watford player. Having made it to the 1984 F. A. Cup Final, where they lost to Everton, Watford proved that they are a club with potential.

'I enjoyed living in the area as well. Not that it has been a problem settling in Glasgow. The people are friendly and there is a lot to do.

'I suppose a great many of my fellow professionals in England found it a little strange that I should want to make such a move.

Colin West in his Sunderland days. A QPR defender loses out this time

I think a lot of them probably imagine that life north of the border is vastly different from the south.

'But I would recommend Scotland to anyone. Glasgow is a lively city and the standard of living is as good as anywhere in England.

'Of course, being the first to reverse the transfer trend meant I was probably under the microscope a bit more when I first arrived at Ibrox.

'But when you look around and realise just how impressive the set-up is, a transfer to Rangers is as big a deal for any player as one to the likes of Liverpool or Manchester United.

'I must confess that I wasn't too well informed on the history of Rangers when I came here at first. As I said earlier, both Ally McCoist and John McClelland had told me a lot about the club and I was aware of Rangers' place on the Scottish football stage. But it's only now that I realise just how great Rangers are in world football terms. The club's fan appeal is really quite remarkable with supporters' associations in just about every part of the globe.

'At the time of my joining Rangers I was staggered to learn that more than 40,000 had turned out for an Old Firm match, even though it was only the Glasgow Cup Final. But that statistic didn't seem to surprise anyone else and now I know why.

'I couldn't wait for the season to get underway just to experience the atmosphere at Ibrox on match day and I wasn't disappointed. In fact, it was nerve-wracking waiting to make my first appearance. I knew people were expecting a lot from me and I was anxious not to let the fans down.

'But I needn't have worried. They gave me a marvellous reception and I was made to feel at home from the first kick of the match. Hopefully, that relationship will continue to prosper.

'Being a part of the Rangers set-up means you can never relax for a moment or rest on your laurels. Past achievements don't mean much if you are not producing the goods week in week out.

'Of course, it's difficult for any player to maintain consistency throughout the season. There are occasions when you hit a sticky patch for any one of several reasons and it's a question of playing through it and trying not to let your confidence evaporate.

'Strikers are perhaps more prone to going off the boil than players in other positions. If you are among the goals fans naturally expect the run to be kept going. But a knock, a run of bad luck or missed timing can affect the flow. Then you've

Charge! Colin West, Rangers' close-season buy from Watford, bears down on the West Brom goal

simply got to be patient and look for someone else to put the ball in the net.'

West freely admits that one of the major reasons for his willingness to become a Ranger was the lure of playing in Europe.

'I would have jumped at the chance of a move to Ibrox even if Rangers had missed out on a UEFA Cup place,' he stresses. 'But it was an added bonus as far as I was concerned.

'Rangers have a great European tradition established over many years of competition. But I know the present group of players are keen to achieve fresh success under Graeme Souness and Walter Smith. We want to be history men in our own right.'